BATTLES IN A NEW LAND

A SOURCEBOOK ON COLONIAL AMERICA

BATTLES IN A NEW LAND

A SOURCEBOOK ON COLONIAL AMERICA

Edited by Carter Smith

AMERICAN ALBUMS FROM THE COLLECTIONS OF
THE LIBRARY OF CONGRESS

THE MILLBROOK PRESS, *Brookfield, Connecticut*

Cover: "The Indians Delivering the English Captives to Colonel Bouquet," hand-colored engraving by Pierre C. Canot, after Benjamin West, 1776.

Title Page: South view of Crown Point, watercolor by Thomas Davies, 1759.

Contents Page: British soldiers of the 1750s, engraving, nineteenth century.

Back Cover: Plan of Cape Breton and Louisbourg (plate II), map in watercolor and ink, eighteenth century.

Library of Congress Cataloging-in-Publication Data

Battles in a new land: a sourcebook on colonial America / edited by
    Carter Smith.
            p. cm. -- (American albums from the collections of the Library of
    Congress)
        Includes bibliographical references and index.
        Summary: Describes and illustrates through contemporary images
    the struggles and conflicts between the European colonizers in America
    as each group sought to dominate the rich New World.
        ISBN 1-56294-034-1
        1. United States--History--Colonial period, ca. 1600-1775--Juvenile
    literature. 2. United States--History--Colonial period, ca. 1600-1775--
    Sources--Juvenile literature. 3. United States--History--Colonial period,
    ca. 1600-1775--Pictorial works--Juvenile literature. 4. United States--
    History, Military--To 1900--Juvenile literature. 5. United States--
    History, Military--To 1900--Sources--Juvenile literature. 6. United
    States--History, Military--To 1900--Pictorial works--Juvenile literature.
    [1. United States--History--Colonial period, ca. 1600-1775--Sources.] I.
    Smith, C. Carter. II. Series.
    E188.B38   1991
    973.2--dc20   91-13940
                                                                  CIP
                                                                  AC

 Created in association with Media Projects Incorporated

C. Carter Smith, *Executive Editor*
Lelia Wardwell, *Managing Editor*
Charles A. Wills, *Consulting Editor*
Kimberly Horstman, *Researcher*
Lydia Link, *Designer*
Athena Angelos, *Photo Researcher*

The consultation of Bernard F. Reilly, Jr., Head Curator of the
Prints and Photographs Division of the Library of Congress, is
gratefully acknowledged.

10 9 8 7 6 5 4 3 2

Contents

King Philip (?-1676) was the chief of the Wampanoag (also known as Pokanoket) tribe, which lived in Massachusetts. Whereas his father, Chief Massasoit, had maintained peace with the Plymouth settlers for decades, King Philip led one of the longest and most decisive wars between the settlers and the Indians—King Philip's War, which began in 1675. This engraving is based on an illustration by Paul Revere.

Introduction

BATTLES IN A NEW LAND is one of the initial volumes in a series published by the Millbrook Press titled AMERICAN ALBUMS FROM THE COLLECTIONS OF THE LIBRARY OF CONGRESS, and one of six books in the series subtitled SOURCEBOOKS ON COLONIAL AMERICA. They treat the early history of our homeland from its discovery and early settlement through the colonial and Revolutionary wars.

The editors' basic goal for the series is to make available to the student many of the original visual documents preserved in the Library of Congress as records of the American past. BATTLES IN A NEW LAND reproduces many of the prints, broadsides, maps, and other original works preserved in the Library's special collections divisions, and a few from its general book collections.

Featured particularly in this volume are the rich holdings of early maps and atlases in the Geography and Maps Division, one of the world's finest archives of eighteenth-century American cartography. Great momentum was given to the Library's collecting in this area by the acquisition in 1867 of the Peter Force Collection of early Americana. This included many of the major early atlases of Delisle, Jefferys, Des Barres, and others. The Library has also amassed over 300 original manuscript military plans produced by British officers during the French and Indian War and the American Revolution, many of these from the working collection of Robert Faden, the foremost English map publisher of the last quarter of the eighteenth century.

The collections reflect the dramatic expansion of the colonial power's knowledge of the coast and interior of North America and the West Indies during the the latter half of the eighteenth century. Improvement in the quality and detail of this knowledge of these regions came with the production of such monuments as Joseph F. W. Des Barres's mammoth navigational atlas of the North American coast, *The Atlantic Neptune,* produced between 1774 and 1778, and Fry Jefferson's 1751 map of the middle and southern colonies. The campaigns of the French and Indian War and colonial disputes were carried on with surprisingly little topographical intelligence, and much of this cartographic activity was prompted by the British and French territorial disputes that led to these conflicts. The 1763 Treaty of Paris, in turn, led to another surge in mapping of the new territorial alignments to come out of those wars.

Aside from the maps, also reproduced here are original engravings and woodcuts, as well as illustrations found in the early published chronicles of colonial history from the Library's other special collections. Political satires such as the comic allegory celebrating British victory in America are from the extensive holdings of English popular prints included in the Windsor Library collection. The engravings in Theodore de Bry's *Historia Americae,* and those in Thomas Hariot's *A Briefe and True Report of the New Found Land of Virginia,* are eyewitness portrayals of colonial events from the Library's rich rare book holdings.

In all, the documents reproduced here represent a small but telling portion of the rich pictorial record of the American past that the Library of Congress preserves in its role as the national library.

BERNARD F. REILLY, JR.

The European colonization of North America was not a peaceful affair. Soon after the first landings in the New World, forests that had heard the war cries of Indians for centuries echoed with a new sound—the roar of European guns.

There were three types of conflict in North America during these years. First, there was conflict between Indian groups, which European settlers quickly exploited for their own benefit. In the land that became New France, for example, Samuel de Champlain sided with the Hurons in their war against the Iroquois, and English settlers in New England learned to play hostile tribes off one another.

The second type of conflict was between settlers and Indians. Despite the best efforts of both groups, there were few places where colonists and Indians lived together peacefully. The differences between European settlers and Indians—differences of language, religion, and way of life—were simply too great. And the European hunger for land pushed Indians throughout North America into a series of desperate conflicts.

Both sides had advantages in these wars. The settlers had firearms. The Indians knew the land and how to fight in it. But the settlers had an invisible but powerful weapon—disease. Unfamiliar diseases brought by the settlers wiped out many once-powerful tribes.

Finally, there was the conflict between rival groups of settlers. Religion as well as nationalism played a part in these battles, as in the Spanish massacre of French Protestants in Florida in 1565. By the middle of the seventeenth century, war between rival European colonies dominated the battlegrounds of Colonial America.

In the spring of 1541, Spanish explorer Hernando de Soto attacked and captured the Indian fortified town at Alibamo, on the Yazoo River in what is now Mississippi. Following this victory, De Soto went on to explore territory west of the Mississippi River. This sketch of the battle appeared in a seventeenth-century history of the Spanish discovery and conquest of America.

A TIMELINE OF MAJOR EVENTS

PART I *1500-1676 Explorations and Rivalries in the New World*

1 5 0 0 - 1 5 4 3

WORLD HISTORY

1502 All Arabs who have not become Christians are expelled from Spain.

Martin Luther

1510 Portugal founds the first European colony in India, at Goa.

1517 German monk Martin Luther protests abuses in the Roman Catholic church, beginning the Protestant Reformation.

1519 Charles I of Spain becomes ruler of the Holy Roman Empire.

1520 Suleiman I, "The Magnificent," becomes Sultan of Turkey.

1521 The army of Suleiman I occupies the European city of Belgrade.

1526 The Mogul dynasty is established in India.

1534 The English Parliament passes The Act of Supremacy, acknowledging Henry VIII as head of the Church of England and beginning the English Reformation.

1539 French army surgeon Ambroise Paré improves the design of artificial limbs for those who have had limbs amputated in battle.

1543 Astronomer Nicolaus Copernicus publishes his *On the Revolution of the Heavenly Spheres*, proposing that the sun, not the earth, is the center of the universe.

COLONIAL HISTORY BATTLES AND CONFLICTS

1508 Juan Ponce de León captures the island of Puerto Rico for Spain.

1520 On the Mexican coast, Hernando Cortés, the Spanish conquistador, defeats troops sent to discipline him. The troops, led by Pánfilo de Nárvaez, have been sent from Cuba by Governor Velasquez.

1521 Juan Ponce de León lands in Florida with 200 men and is wounded in an attack by Indians. He returns to Cuba, where he dies.
•Hernando Cortés defeats the army of Aztec emperor Montezuma and takes Mexico's capital, the city of Tenochtitlan.

1539 Searching for land and gold, the governor of Cuba, Hernando de Soto, arrives in Florida at Tampa Bay with 600 soldiers. They march through parts of Alabama, Arkansas, Georgia, South Carolina, and Tennessee, ravaging local Indian tribes, including the Apalachee and Creek.

1540 Believing it to be one of the legendary "Seven Cities of Gold" (Cibola), Francisco Vásquez de Coronado seizes a Zuñi Indian pueblo at Hawikuh in New Mexico.

1542 Spanish explorer and soldier Hernando de Soto dies beside the "great muddy river," the Mississippi, which he has discovered just over a year ago. He is forty-six years old.

COLONIAL HISTORY GOVERNMENT

1507 German mapmaker Martin Waldseemuller uses the name "America" on a new map of the world, applying it to the New World continent that he shows lying between Europe and Asia. He takes the word from the name of Italian merchant Amerigo Vespucci, who claims to have discovered the mainland of the New World in 1497, a year before Christopher Columbus. The claim is disputed, but the name sticks.

1510 Vasco Núñez de Balboa founds the Spanish settlement of Darien, on the Atlantic coast of the isthmus of Panama.

1514 Bartolomé de Las Casas, the first priest ordained in the New World, returns to Spain to urge the abolition of Indian slavery in the West Indies.

1518 King Charles I of Spain allows Africans to be imported to the West Indies as slaves.

1533 The Spanish Governor of Peru, Francisco Pizzaro, executes the last Incan emperor, Atahualpa. Pizzaro has collected a huge ransom for the Incan, but then claims his death is necessary to assure Spain's rule in Peru.

1539 Antonio de Mendoza, First Viceroy of Mexico, establishes the New World's first printing press, in Mexico City.

1540 Francisco de Coroñado sets out to explore the lands north of Mexico with a company of cavalry and 1,000 horses, introducing the horse to North America.

1546 The Catholic Countereformation begins. It attempts to reverse the gains made by Protestantism.

1547 Ivan IV, "The Terrible," is crowned Czar of Russia.

1554 Queen Mary of England restores that nation to Catholicism.

1557 Portugal founds the colony of Macao on the Chinese coast.

1559 Elizabeth I becomes Queen of England, making the nation Protestant again.

Sixteenth-century Spanish ships

1562 The Wars of Religion between French Catholics and Protestants (Huguenots) begin.

1566 Protestants in the Netherlands revolt against Catholic rule.

1572 English sea captain Francis Drake attacks Spanish harbors and loots Spanish ships.

1588 The Spanish Armada sails from Spain hoping to conquer

England: the fleet is destroyed by a combination of English warships and storms.

1594 Prince Henry of Navarre becomes King Henry IV of France.

1595 The Dutch East India Company sends trading expeditions to Asia.

1565 Intent on removing the French from Florida, a Spanish force led by Pedro Menéndez de Avilés captures Fort Caroline (located in what is now South Carolina) and kills all but a handful of the French Huguenot settlers. Menéndez renames the fort San Mateo and builds a string of other forts to defend Spanish claims to the region.

1580 Marques defeats a

French fleet led by Gilberto Gil, who is killed in battle, marking the end of French influence in Florida.

1586 English sea captain Sir Francis Drake attacks and burns Santiago in the Cape Verde Islands, holds the city of San Domingo (Dominica) for ransom, captures and ransoms Cartagena (Colombia), and burns the Spanish settlement at St. Augustine in Florida. To

the Spanish, he is known as "El Draque" ("The Dragon").

1591 Sir Richard Grenville, founder of the Roanoke colony, is killed in a sea battle with the Spanish off the Azores.

1593 A Spanish expedition, led by Francisco de Levya Bonilla and Antonio Gutierez de Humana, is wiped out by Indians in the region now known as Kansas.

The expedition has been seeking gold.

Sir Francis Drake

1551 A new law forbids blacks in New Spain from marrying Indians or carrying guns.

1552 Spanish Dominican friar Bartolomé de Las Casas publishes a bitter attack on the brutality of Spanish government in the New World. He calls his book *Brief Relations of the Destruction of the Indies*.

1565 Spanish Admiral Pedro Menéndez de

Avilés establishes a colony at St. Augustine, Florida.

1570 Five Iroquois tribes, the Mohawk, Onondaga, Oneida, Cayuga, and Seneca, form a confederation. Delegates to the confederation are chosen by women.

1579 English seafarer Francis Drake discovers San Francisco Bay.

Totem of the Five Iroquois Nations

1584 Sir Walter Raleigh discovers Virginia and names it for England's Queen Elizabeth I, "The Virgin Queen."

1587 The first English child in the New World is born at the Roanoke colony in Virginia. She is named Virginia Dare.

1598 The Marquis de la Roche leaves forty French convicts on Sable Island, off the coast of Nova Scotia.

A TIMELINE OF MAJOR EVENTS

PART I *1500-1676 Explorations and Rivalries in the New Land*

1 6 0 3 - 1 6 3 7

WORLD HISTORY

1603 Queen Elizabeth I of England dies and is succeeded by King James I. He is already King of Scotland (as James VI), and thus unites the two countries.

1605 Boris Godunov, Czar of Russia, dies.
•Akbar the Great, Mogul emperor of India, dies.

1606 A Portuguese expedition led by Luis Vaez Torres sights the west coast of Australia.

1608 A royal decree issued in Spain legalizes the enslavement of Chile's Indians.

1621 The Dutch West India Company is founded.
•Foreign travel is declared a capital offense in Japan.

1629 King James I of England dies and is succeeded by Charles I.

1630 Gustavus Adolphus, king of Sweden, invades the Holy Roman Empire; he is killed in battle two years later.

1633 Christians are persecuted in Japan under the Exclusion Decree.

1637 Russian explorers cross Siberia and reach the Pacific Ocean.

Gustavus Adolphus

COLONIAL HISTORY BATTLES AND CONFLICTS

1611 Military rule is established in Jamestown in an attempt to save the colony through harsh discipline.

1613 Sir Samuel Argall sails from Jamestown and destroys the French outpost at Port Royal, Nova Scotia. He captures the outpost at Mount Desert Island, Maine, and returns to Virginia with fifteen French prisoners.

1622 Indians led by Opechancanough massacre some 350 of the 1,200 colonists at Jamestown, Virginia.

1636 Pequot Indians kill a New England trader named John Oldham, which leads to a series of attacks by colonists against the Pequots who live in the Rhode Island, Long Island, and Connecticut regions.
•Massachusetts governor John Endecott creates a military force to pursue and punish the Pequot Indians.

1637 Forces under Captain John Mason slaughter men, women, and children at the main Pequot camp near Stonington, Connecticut.
•Near Fairfield, Connecticut, a force of Massachusetts Bay, Plymouth, and Connecticut colonists massacre what remains of the Pequots.

1628 The Plymouth colonists send Miles Standish to destroy the Merrymount settlement led by Thomas Morton at Quincy, Massachusetts. Morton is sent back to England on charges of selling arms to the Indians and harboring runaway servants.

COLONIAL HISTORY GOVERNMENT

1607 English settlers establish a colony at Jamestown, Virginia.
•Captain John Smith of the Jamestown colony is captured by Powhatan, leader of a powerful confederacy of Virginian Indians. His life is saved by Pocahontas, Powhatan's daughter.

1608 French explorer Samuel de Champlain sets up a trading post at Quebec and achieves friendly relations with the Huron Indians by helping them fight their enemy, the Iroquois.

1609 Champlain, guided by Huron and Algonquin Indians, explores the lake later named for him.

1616 A smallpox epidemic, brought by European settlers, kills many New England Indians.

1621 The Plymouth settlers sign a peace pact with the Wampanoag Indians.

1624 The colony of New Amsterdam is founded by the Dutch West India Company on the southern tip of present day Manhattan Island.

Houses in New Amsterdam

1641 Japan bans all foreigners except for Dutch traders, who are confined to a man-made island in Nagasaki harbor.

1642 The English Civil War begins. The conflict is between the supporters of Charles I and the Church of England and the largely Puritan supporters of Parliamentary government.

1646 The English Civil War ends with the

defeat of Charles I and the Royalists. Three years later King Charles is executed.

Execution of Charles I

1648 The Peace of Westphalia ends the Thirty Years War

1651 Charles II, son of the executed Charles I of England, is crowned king of Scotland. He invades England without success and flees to France.

1652 England declares war on Holland.

1654 The Treaty of Westminster ends the first Anglo-Dutch War.

1659 The Treaty of the Pyrenees ends the war between France and Spain; France becomes the dominant power in Europe.

1660 The English monarchy is restored, with Charles II as King.

1668 England, Holland and Sweden form the Triple Alliance to oppose the French seizure of the Spanish Netherlands.

1644 Indians in Virginia rise up against the settlers. After two years the Indians are defeated and forced to give up all their land between the James and York Rivers.

1651 The Dutch build Fort Casimir on the Delaware River, giving them control of the routes into Swedish territory. The Swedes attack and capture Fort Casimir.

1655 A Dutch force led

by Peter Stuyvesant recaptures Fort Casimir. The victory ends Sweden's claims in America.

1664 Richard Nicolls, acting for the Duke of York, arrives in New York Harbor with several warships. He forces Peter Stuyvesant to surrender the Dutch territory of New Netherland, and renames New Amsterdam New York.

1673 A Dutch fleet wins

back the territory of New Netherland.

Stuyvesant surrendering

1675 Plymouth colonists execute three Wampanoag Indians and provoke King Philip's War.
•Indians led by King Philip achieve a victory at Bloody Brook, near Deerfield, Massachusetts.
•A combined colonial force defeats the Narragansett Indians near Kingston, Rhode Island, killing over 300 women and children.

1645 The Dutch and Hudson River Valley Indians declare peace. In Boston, a peace treaty is signed between the New England Confederation and the Narrangansett Indians.

Early view of New Amsterdam

1652 The Massachusetts Bay Company takes over Maine and declares itself independent of the English Parliament.

1653 New Amsterdam (later New York) incor-

porates as a city with 800 residents.

1654 English colonists capture Acadia (Nova Scotia) from the French.

1663 Charles II, King of England, grants Carolina to eight wealthy proprietors.

1664 King Charles grants his brother, the Duke of York, all land from Maine to Delaware not already settled by English colonists.

1665 The colony of New Jersey is founded.

1668 Jesuit Father Jacques Marquette founds a mission at Sault Ste. Marie in present-day Michigan.

1674 The Treaty of Westminster between England and the Netherlands recognizes the settlers of New York and New Sweden as English subjects.

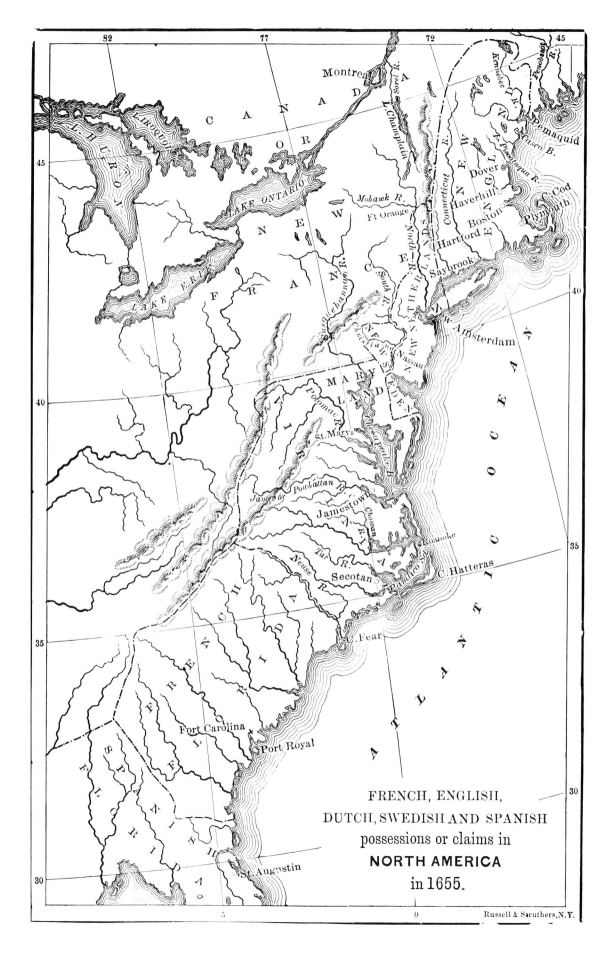

FRENCH, ENGLISH,
DUTCH, SWEDISH AND SPANISH
possessions or claims in
NORTH AMERICA
in 1655.

The Colonies in 1655

In 1655, the greatest power in the New World east of the Mississippi River, in terms of territory, was France. With its capital at Quebec, New France included the St. Lawrence River country, the Great Lakes region, most of the land between the Mississippi River and the Allegheny Mountains, plus much of what would become the Carolinas (called "French Florida" on the map). The French had good relations with a number of Indian groups, especially the Hurons, whom they relied on to hold back the powerful Iroquois Confederacy in the lands south of Lake Ontario. However, New France's European population was small—only a few thousand in 1655—and its economy was based largely on fur trading and fishing.

In contrast, the English colonies had a growing population and a diverse economy by 1655. The English colonies were divided into two regions: New England (mainly the Massachusetts Bay Colony, but including settlements in Rhode Island, Connecticut, and outlying areas) and the tidewater of Chesapeake Bay (Virginia and Maryland).

Dividing New England from the southern colonies was New Netherland. This Dutch colony, with its capital at New Amsterdam on Manhattan Island, stretched north along the Hudson River Valley and south to Chesapeake Bay. In 1655, New Netherland captured and absorbed New Sweden, the small Swedish colony in the Delaware River Valley.

Finally, to the south of Virginia and French Florida was Spanish Florida—Spain's remaining colony in eastern North America. Spain had been the first nation to explore North America, but by the mid-1600s, its colonial efforts were centered on South and Central America and the lands west of the Mississippi River.

THE SPANISH CONQUERORS

The discovery of America began with a long line of Spanish explorers. Between 1492 and 1504, Christopher Columbus explored much of the Caribbean. In 1513, Vasco Núñez de Balboa explored the isthmus of Panama, reaching the Pacific Ocean. Juan Ponce de León discovered the Florida mainland. From 1519 to 1521, Hernando Cortés and his band of adventurers conquered the Mexican empire ruled by Aztec leader Montezuma. Beginning in 1539, Hernando de Soto traveled through much of northern Florida and parts of what would become the southeast United States. He landed at Tampa Bay in 1539 in search of riches and fame. De Soto traveled the Arkansas River and discovered the Mississippi River. In these travels, he encountered local Indian tribes—the Timucua, the Apalachee, the Creek, and others. Because he mistreated the Indians so badly, torturing them and stealing from them, the once-friendly Indians became hostile and many battles broke out. After De Soto died in 1542, his conquests were reported by the seventeenth-century Spanish chronicler Antonio de Herrera. De Soto's burial in the Mississippi River is recounted in these words:

> With Florida his conquests were not stayed.
> For such a death shall no tomb be made:
> Let the Great River keep him in its ward...

De Soto (c. 1500-42; above) began his journey through the south in 1539 in search of riches and fertile land. He continued through the southeast, exploring what is now Alabama, Arkansas, Georgia, South Carolina, and Tennessee, and the "Father of the Waters"—the Mississippi River. De Soto died of a fever on May 21, 1542, and was buried in the Mississippi.

De Soto and his soldiers attacked many of the Indians they encountered in their travels. This engraving by Theodore de Bry (opposite page, above) shows a particularly brutal assault. Upon meeting De Soto, the Indians welcomed him, but he did not return their kindness. He took their food, their valuables, their women, and a guide to lead him to the next town.

For De Soto, as for many explorers, Florida was an early stop. On June 25, 1539, with a fleet of seven ships, he landed at Tampa Bay. This engraving (right) is a nineteenth-century view of De Soto's camp in Florida.

RIVALRY IN FLORIDA: THE FRENCH VS. THE SPANISH

In the 1560s, Spain was near the height of its power as a builder of empires. Its explorers and *conquistadores* had traveled throughout the world, winning territory stretching from the Caribbean to the Philippines. This monopoly was then challenged by the French, who explored the coast of Florida. In 1562, the Frenchman Jean Ribaut tried to establish a settlement near the site of what is now Jacksonville, Florida. In 1564, René de Laudonnière returned to the area explored by Ribaut and established a fort, Fort Caroline. For much of the time they were there, the French depended for their survival on the local Indian tribes, like the Timucuas. Without their help, the first group of settlers would not have survived their first winter.

The French lasted at Fort Caroline until 1565, when the Spanish attacked the fort and killed all remaining settlers. Upon meeting the French at the entry to the fort, the Spanish leader is said to have announced: "I am the general. My name is Pedro Menéndez de Avilés. This is the armada of the King of Spain, who has sent me to this coast and country to burn and hang the Lutheran French who should be found there." But the true test of the Spanish empire came from the English, in the person of the explorer Sir Francis Drake.

The French made alliances with local Indians, like the Timucuas of northern Florida. The leader of the Timucuas, Chief Outina, became involved in a battle, shown in this engraving (opposite page, top) by Theodore de Bry, with Chief Potanou and his forces. Chief Outina enlisted the help of French soldiers, called harquebusiers *because of their gun, the* harquebus. *Without their help, Chief Outina would not have defeated his enemy.*

Like their European counterparts in the New World, warring Indian tribes sometimes destroyed their enemy's villages. Their method was to approach the town quietly and shoot arrows covered with burning moss onto village rooftops, as this engraving (opposite page, bottom), also by De Bry, illustrates. The roofs, which were made of dried palm, burned quickly. Sometimes the huts were completely destroyed. While the huts burned, the attacking Indians escaped.

Relations between the French settlers and their Indian allies were not always friendly. In some cases, jealousy and competition among the groups resulted in bloodshed, as shown in this De Bry engraving (opposite page, bottom). Pierre Gambié was a wealthy local trader and husband of a local chief's daughter. For a visit to friends at Fort Caroline, he arranged to have two Indians accompany him in a canoe, in which he had stashed his trading fortune. While Gambié bent over to make a fire, he was killed by the Indians.

In the late 1500's, England and Spain fought fiercely for power in the New World. In 1585, Sir Francis Drake (c. 1540-96) was sent on a mission to destroy Spanish settlements. One stop was St. Augustine, Florida, which was held by the Spanish. Upon arrival, he ordered his soldiers to burn the town and claim it for the English. This map (below), from a sixteenth-century book on Drake's expeditions, shows his naval attack.

In 1562, Jean Ribaut (c. 1520-65) found a site on the St. John's River for a colony of French Huguenots, who were seeking religious freedom. In 1564, a lieutenant of Ribaut's, René de Laudonnière, built a fort for the colony, named Fort Caroline. In 1565, the Spanish arrived, planning to claim the land. Led by Pedro Menéndez de Avilés, the Spanish troops massacred the defenseless Huguenots and took the fort. The Spanish renamed the fort San Mateo. The massacre is portrayed in this illustration from the nineteenth century.

THE FRENCH COME TO THE NORTH: SAMUEL DE CHAMPLAIN

Following their unsuccessful attempts to colonize the southeast, the French shifted their efforts to the north. They decided to settle in territory untouched by the Spanish, the land that became Canada. Like the Spanish, they first looked for a passage to the Orient, where they hoped to develop trading. What they found instead was a huge land and a lucrative trade in the beaver pelts (fur).

One of the most famous French settlers and explorers was Samuel de Champlain. Champlain established his first trading post in 1608 near what would become the city of Quebec. To regulate beaver trapping, he started the system of company monopolies. But most important to the success of trapping and trading beaver pelts were his relations with the local Indians. Champlain cooperated closely with local Indians, learning their habits and dialects. He became governor of the colony of New France. He inspired a generation of explorers of the region, which led to more colonization. He was also an important chronicler of the people of the land in which he traveled. His maps and illustrations of Indians are still prized as a source of information about colonial North America.

LES
VOYAGES
DE LA
NOVVELLE FRANCE
OCCIDENTALE, DICTE
CANADA,
FAITS PAR LE S' DE CHAMPLAIN
Xainctongeois, Capitaine pour le Roy en la Marine du
Ponant, & toutes les Defcouuertes qu'il a faites en
ce païs depuis l'an 1603. iufques en l'an 1629.
Où fe voit comme ce pays a efté premierement defcouuert par les François,
fous l'authorité de nos Roys tres-Chreftiens, iufques au regne
de fa Majefté à prefent regnant LOVIS XIII.
Roy de France & de Nauarre.
Auec vn traitté des qualitez & conditions requifes à vn bon & parfaict Nauigateur
pour cognoiftre la diuerfité des Eftimes qui fe font en la Nauigation. Les
Marques & enfeignemens que la prouidence de Dieu à mifes dans les Mers
pour redreffer les Mariniers en leur routte, fans lefquelles ils tomberoient en
de grands dangers, Et la maniere de bien dreffer Cartes marines auec leurs
Ports, Rades, Ifles, Sondes, & autre chofe neceffaire à la Nauigation.
Enfemble vne Carte generalle de la defcription dudit pays faite en fon Meridien felon
la declinaifon de la guide Aymant, & vn Catechifme ou Inftruction traduitte
du François au langage des peuples Sauuages de quelque contrée, auec
ce qui s'eft paffé en ladite Nouuelle France en l'année 1651.
A MONSEIGNEVR LE CARDINAL DVC DE RICHELIEV.

A PARIS.
Chez PIERRE LE-MVR, dans la grand' Salle
du Palais.

M. DC. XXXII.
Auec Priuilege du Roy.

Champlain wanted to explore Canada to find a northwest passage to the Orient and to set up a base for fur trading. In Les Voyages de La Nouvelle France *(above), he describes his eight voyages, his encounters with Indians, and his navigational experiences. He shows himself to be what he later called a "Good Captain": "An upright, God-fearing man . . . with good sea-legs . . . knowing everything that concerns the handling of the ship."*

This map of "Nouvelle France" (below) shows the land Samuel de Champlain (c. 1567-1635) explored in his many years of travel. It includes most of the Great Lakes, the lower peninsula of Michigan, the Detroit River, and the falls ("Sault") on the strait between Lakes Huron and Superior. Note the map's careful precision in showing areas inhabited by Indians ("Algommequins," "Hirocois") and animals ("beuffles," or buffalo).

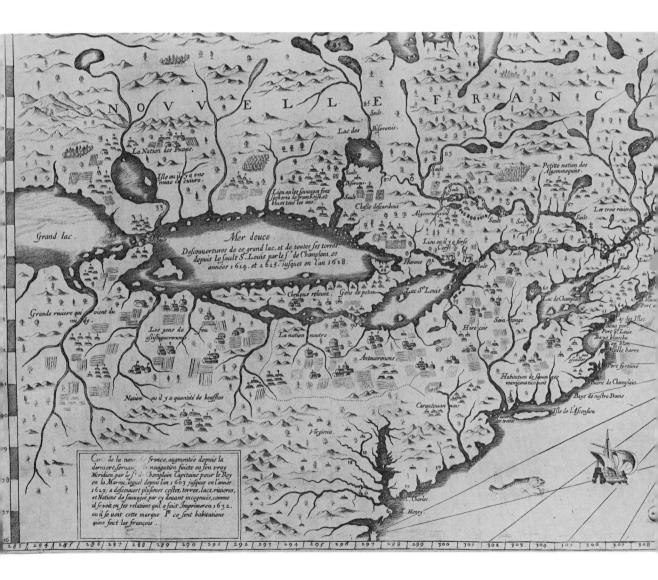

CHAMPLAIN AND THE NORTHERN INDIANS

There were constant struggles for power between the Five Nations of the Iroquois Confederacy and other tribes, including the Hurons of the Ottawa River Valley and the Montagnais, who lived in the St. Lawrence River Valley. Champlain helped the Hurons and Montagnais fight the Iroquois. He won their trust and they acted as go-betweens for the French in the fur trade, which was centered in Montreal. Originally a Huron village located on an island in the St. Lawrence River, Montreal was first discovered by Jacques Cartier in 1535. Champlain visited the island in 1603, but it was not settled until 1642 by the French. Because of its fine harbor and its position on the St. Lawrence River, Montreal became a vital trading center.

Champlain needed the help of the Hurons and the Montagnais to insure smooth trading. In 1624, the Iroquois fought back by ambushing a fleet of Huron canoes carrying fur to Montreal. Champlain had allied himself with the weaker of the Indian tribes. His allies were numerous, but they were not as able warriors as the Iroquois, who lived in the land south of Lake Ontario in what is now New York. In the second half of the seventeenth century, the English began to settle on the Hudson and Mohawk rivers in New York, so they were natural allies of the native Iroquois. Eventually, the union between the English and the Iroquois helped to destroy the French colonies.

On the evening of July 29, 1609, Champlain, a few French soldiers, and sixty Montagnais and Huron Indians prepared to battle two hundred Iroquois. At dawn, Champlain scared the Iroquois with something they had never seen before—his shiny suit of armor and musket. Champlain's troops overwhelmed the Iroquois. The victory strengthened the alliance between the French and the Algonquins. This illustration from Champlain's book (above) shows the surprise attack.

Unlike European soldiers, who wore a suit of half-armor and an open-faced metal helmet, the Iroquois warrior wore a slatted wooden body armor and carried a wooden shield. This sketch (left) appears in Champlain's book.

In July 1609, the French and Algonquins fought the Iroquois in what is now known as the Battle of Lake Champlain. The French and Algonquin fighters used two types of weapons: the musket and the bow and arrow. They are shown attacking an Iroquois stronghold in this illustration (right), also from Champlain's book.

The fur trade was a source of wealth for the Iroquois. When the French allied with the Hurons, they gained control of the fur trade, a shift that the Iroquois resented. This nineteenth-century engraving (below) shows Europeans and Indians trading in beaver pelts. There was a high demand in Europe for the pelts, which were pressed into felt and used for hats.

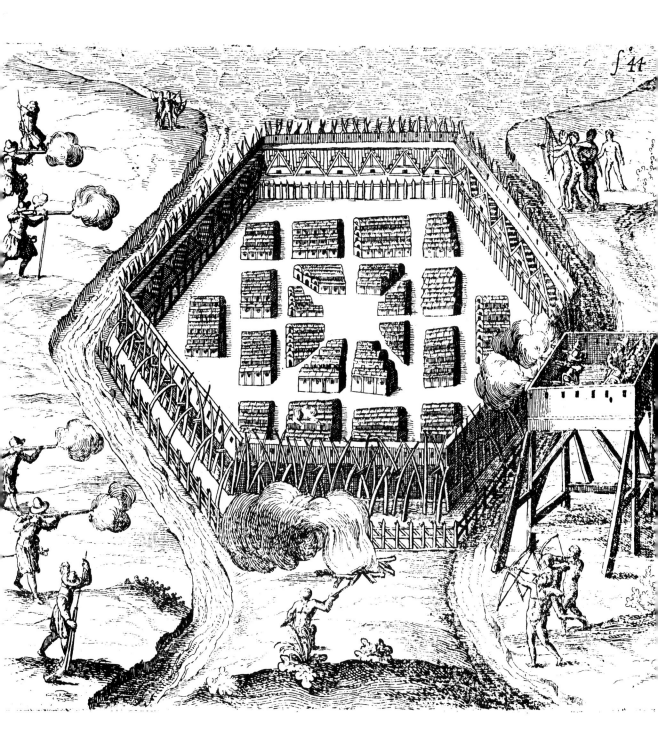

FRENCH JESUITS AND CANADIAN INDIANS

Although New France was an active region for trading, its first permanent settlers were missionaries. In 1610 and 1611, Roman Catholic missionaries attempted two ambitious but unsuccessful settlements. One was founded by a self-proclaimed missionary who did not follow the rules of any church. The second was run by a French Jesuit whose quarrels with the colonial leaders led them to close the mission down.

At the suggestion of Samuel de Champlain, another group of missionaries, the Recollets, traveled to New France in 1615. These missionaries were more successful. They worked among the Montagnais, the Algonquins, and the Hurons. The missionaries learned Indian ways and attempted to convert the Indians to Christianity. They built seminaries to train Indian boys for the priesthood. Generally, the missionaries treated the Indians with respect, if not complete understanding. In return, the Indians were loyal. This peace lasted for several decades until the Iroquois attacked the missions. The difficulties caused by this large and powerful tribe prompted the French missionaries to ask for help from the French crown. In 1664, King Louis XIV took direct control of the colonies.

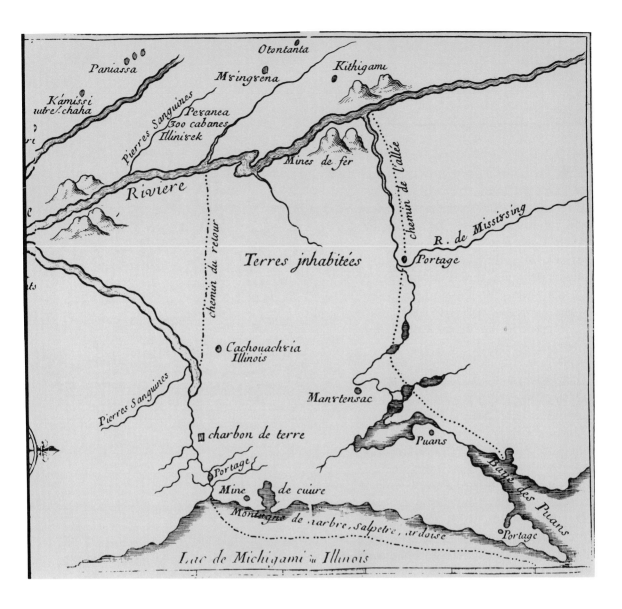

Books about missionary travels among the Indians were popular in France. One such book was Le Grand Voyage du Pays des Hurons (opposite page, top), written in 1632 by Gabriel Sagard-Théodat, a brother in the Recollect order.

The almost-naked Indian warrior (opposite page, bottom) appeared in a history of Canada written by a Jesuit priest in 1664.

Champlain inspired many explorers to visit the Great Lakes area. Probably the first explorer to see the forests of Michigan was Étienne Brulé, a fur trader. The first to pass the Straits of Mackinac and visit what is now Wisconsin was Jean Nicolet. In the late seventeenth century, the Jesuits set up communities in Michigan. This led to Father Jacques Marquette's famous explorations of the Mississippi River regions, shown in this seventeenth-century French map (above).

TENSIONS AND ALLIANCES IN VIRGINIA

In May 1607, the first permanent English settlement in North America was established at Jamestown. There was much dissent among the settlers. One of the group's main leaders was Captain John Smith, whose expeditions into Indian territory brought him respect. One of his most important encounters was with Powhatan, leader of the powerful Powhatan Confederacy of Indian tribes.

On some occasions Indian tribes ambushed the English settlers. Chief Powhatan grudgingly recognized the benefits of establishing friendly relations with the English. In 1614, when his daughter, Pocahontas, was married to Englishman John Rolfe, Powhatan maintained a lasting peace with the settlers. This changed when Powhatan died in 1617 and his brother Opechancanough took over leadership of the tribes. Opechancanough feared that English interest in Indian land and their desire to Christianize Indian children meant they wanted to control the Indians. This led to several Indian attacks, including the Jamestown massacre of 1622, in which over a quarter of the Jamestown settlers were killed.

This engraving (above), by Theodore de Bry, shows the Indian village at Pomeiock. Fortified with long poles stuck into the ground, the town had only one narrow entrance.

In some colonies, chiefs, such as the one pictured here (opposite page, bottom), and colonial officials made peace and had separate governments. In other settlements, the arrangement was not so peaceful. Settlers would request that Indian chiefs subordinate themselves to the colonial lord's jurisdiction.

Powhatan, the sachem, or leader, of several Tidewater Virginia tribes, was so powerful that the settlers felt he was a kind of king. Disputes often broke out. In one case, Captain John Smith (c. 1580-1631) was captured by Powhatan, but was released (according to Smith) at the request of Powhatan's daughter, Pocahontas. This confrontation between Smith and Powhatan (opposite page, top) is a detail from a 1624 map.

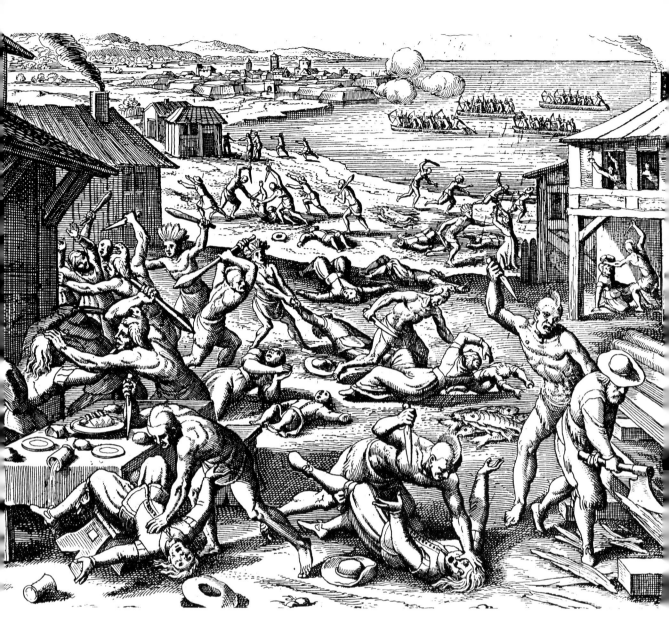

The Jamestown Massacre was one of the most violent encounters between settlers and Indians. On March 22, 1622, Indian warriors led by Opechancanough struck the Jamestown settlement without warning, as shown in this De Bry engraving (above). They killed 347 of its 1,200 inhabitants. One friendly Indian informed Jamestown settlers that they were in danger. These settlers destroyed the Indians' crops and villages. Fighting continued for several years.

In 1644, twenty-two years after the Jamestown massacre, Opech-ancanough led a different group of Indians, the Pamunkeys, into Jamestown. They raided the town and killed three hundred of the eight thousand settlers. This time, Opechancanough did not escape. Shortly after his capture, Opechancanough died in prison. In this engraving (below), his body is being taken for burial, as Jamestown citizens look on.

MILES STANDISH AND THE PILGRIMS

The Pilgrims founded their colony in Plymouth in 1620. These colonists were fleeing religious persecution in England. The Pilgrims were fortunate to establish friendly relations with the Indians. At first, the settlers and the Indians shared knowledge and goods. At the center of these relations was the Pilgrims' adviser in "foreign relations," Miles Standish. Standish was a short, sturdy soldier of fortune who was hired by the Pilgrims to accompany them on their journey from London. Standish soon became adept at working with the Indians. He learned their dialects and put an end to early Indian attack plans. He was among the Pilgrims who negotiated a peace treaty with Massasoit, chief of the Wampanoags. This treaty said, in part:

> 1. That neither he [Massasoit] nor any of his [people] should injure or do hurt to any of their people.
>
> 2. That if he did hurt any of theirs, he should send the offender, that they might punish him.
>
> 3. That if anything were taken away from any of theirs he should cause it to be restored; and they should do like to his.

Other tribes attacked the colony, but Massasoit kept the peace. The colony did not suffer serious problems until after Massasoit's death in 1661, when his sons became leaders.

A colony of English settlers lived in Wessagusset, Massachusetts, at peace with the local Indians. But Plymouth adviser Miles Standish (c. 1584-1656) believed good relations in Wessagusset would hurt Plymouth's fur trade. When the colonists refused to expel the Indians from the community, Standish himself attacked and killed several Indians, as shown in this nineteenth-century illustration (above).

In December 1620, a party of 102 Pilgrims arrived at Plymouth, Massachusetts. Their first encampment is portrayed in this nineteenth-century illustration (opposite page, bottom). The first Indian who helped them was Tisquantum, also known as Squanto. He advised them to plant corn and squash, showed them how to hunt and fish, and introduced them to Massasoit (?-1661), leader of the Wampanoags.

Soon after the Pilgrims arrived, they negotiated a treaty with the Wampanoags, who were suffering losses from disease and attacks by the Narragansett tribe. The settlers, in turn, needed guidance to survive in the new land. This note (right) from Miles Standish lists expenses for a meeting with the Wampanoag leader, Massasoit.

Gov'r'nrs Bradford

Sir .... My journey to Massasoit's lodge may be worth 16 s. 4 d to your humble servant.

Myles Standish

Plymouth Colonie
16 June 1621.

THE PEQUOT WAR

The Pequots were the most aggressive Indian tribe in New England. Yet for several years after English settlers landed in the Connecticut River Valley, the two groups lived in peace. But when colonists moved farther into Pequot territory, the Pequots became angry. Skirmishes began. In 1634 and 1636, English traders were killed, probably by the Pequots. In 1636, the colonists struck back by destroying a Pequot village. In turn, the Pequots killed several settlers. The Pequot chief, Sassacus, gathered his forces together. In May 1637, full-scale war began. Captain John Mason led the settlers, with allies from the Mohegan and Narragansett tribes, in an attack on the main Pequot village in Connecticut. Several hundred Indians, including women and children, were burned alive. The English lost only two men. Most Indians who escaped death were sold into slavery. Others, including Chief Sassacus, were caught and killed by Indians friendly to the settlers. The Mohegans, who were allies of the English, gained control of Pequot lands. According to Cotton Mather, the Puritan writer and religious leader, the Puritans felt that this war was "a sweet sacrifice, and . . . gave the praise thereof to God." It was the bloodiest fight between the two groups to date.

This map (opposite page, top) shows some of the battle sites of the Pequot War. By the early 1600s, settlers forced the Pequot Indians into a small area, bordered by the Connecticut River and Narragansett Bay. In 1636, angry Pequots killed a Boston trader named John Oldham. Thirty settlers were massacred in Saybrook and Wethersfield. On the Mystic River, colonial forces launched a successful night attack on a Pequot village in 1637.

On May 26, 1637, Captains John Underhill and John Mason and Mohegan Chief Uncas led ninety colonial soldiers, sixty Mohegan Indians, and several hundred Narragansett Indians in an attack on a Pequot fort near West Mystic, Connecticut, portrayed in this diagram (opposite page, bottom). They set the fort on fire, killing hundreds of Pequot warriors and family members. By the end of the Pequot War, the tribe was virtually wiped out.

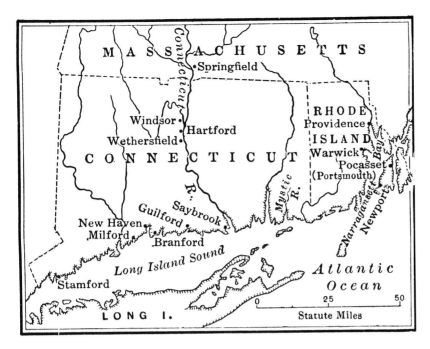

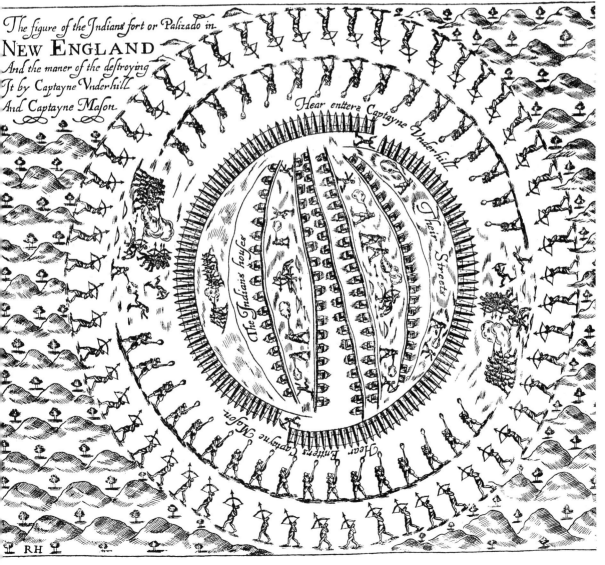

The figure of the Indians fort or Palizado in
NEW ENGLAND
And the maner of the destroying
It by Captayne Vnderhill
And Captayne Mason

Hear enttera Captayne Vnderhill

The Indians houses

Their Streets

Hear Entters Captayne Mason

RH

THE DUTCH AND SWEDISH RIVALRY ON THE DELAWARE

Both the Dutch and the Swedish wanted to make money in the New World through trade. They set up colonies for that purpose. In March 1638, twenty-three Swedish soldiers and two officers of the Swedish West Indian Company founded the colony of New Sweden. It was the first and only permanent settlement by the Swedes. Located on the Delaware River near present-day Wilmington, across from the Dutch colony of New Netherland, it was protected by a fort called Fort Christina, after the Swedish queen. Its strategic location meant that the Swedes controlled trade in the Delaware Valley. In 1643, New Sweden got a new governor, Johan Printz. Although he was a harsh leader, he was successful at keeping peace with the Indians and increasing Swedish trade. For ten years he encouraged Swedish settlement, but he was not popular with the two hundred settlers in New Sweden, and was forced to return to Sweden. In 1654, his replacement, Johan Rising, captured a Dutch fort, Fort Casimir, and renamed it Fort Trinity. Peter Stuyvesant, leader of the New Netherland colony, retaliated in 1655. Stuyvesant led three hundred troops from his settlement of New Netherland to recapture his fort and take Fort Christina. New Sweden had come to an end.

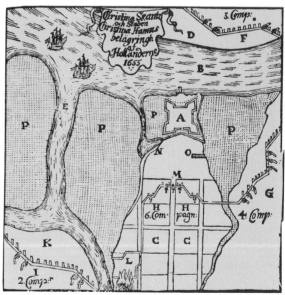

This 1655 map (above) of Fort Christina shows how the Swedish forces tried to protect the area during its siege. The town of Christina Hamn (C) is at the bottom right. It is protected by the Rat Battery (H), the Gnat Battery (G), the Fly Battery (D), and the Snake Battery (F). The Dutch attacked from point M, just outside of town. After a ten-day encounter, the colony surrendered on September 1, 1655.

In the early 1650s, Peter Stuyvesant (1592-1672), Dutch governor of New Amsterdam, built a fort called Casimir shown in this seventeenth-century drawing (left). The Swedish sent Captain Johan Rising to reclaim the colony for Sweden. He landed near Fort Casimir on May 21, 1654. At gunpoint, he demanded that the Dutch surrender. The Dutch were unarmed, and the fort was taken without bloodshed. Rising renamed it Fort Trefaldiget, Swedish for trinity.

This map (right) of the first and only Swedish colony in the New World is dated 1655. At its most populous, it had only four hundred colonists.

Swedish settlers in the Delaware Valley traded with the local Delaware and Susquehannock Indians. In 1643, the Swedish colony provided arms to the Indians, who were at war with a Maryland tribe. They also made alliances with them. A negotiation between the Indians and the Swedes is portrayed in this contemporary engraving (below). They "bought" land to use "for the sake of trade" —for trapping, not for permanent settlement.

THE SURRENDER OF NEW AMSTERDAM

The Dutch and the English were in constant competition for land and trade routes. The English were especially interested in New Amsterdam, present-day New York City. The Dutch colony separated England's New England and southern colonies. It was also an important center for the fur trade. Since 1647, it had been led by Governor Peter Stuyvesant, an explorer and soldier in the service of the Dutch West India Company. In 1644, on St. Martin, in the West Indies, he lost his right leg in battle. He replaced it with a peg leg, which he proudly decorated with silver as a badge of honor. Stuyvesant was a hard man, a tyrannical leader, but he managed to make New Amsterdam a successful Dutch colony.

In 1664, the English took control of the colony. English colonel Richard Nicolls led four ships into the harbor of New Amsterdam and demanded that Stuyvesant surrender the colony. After a dramatic refusal, he surrendered the island to the English. The town of New Amsterdam was renamed New York. This gave England control of an unbroken string of colonies along the Atlantic coast.

CONDITIEN,

Die door de Heeren BVRGERMEESTEREN der Stadt *Amstelredam*, volgens 't gemaeckte Accoordt met de *West-Indische Compagnie*, ende d'Approbatie van hare Hog. Mog. de Heeren STATEN GENERAEL *der Vereenighde Nederlanden*, daer op gevolght, geprefenteert werden aen alle de gene, die als Coloniers na Nieuw-Nederlandt willen vertrecken, &c.

tA M S T E R D A M,

By JAN BANNING, Ordinaris Drucker defer Stede, in 't jaer 1656.

After Stuyvesant took Fort Trinity from the Swedes in 1655, well-to-do Dutch merchants moved from Amsterdam to the new Dutch possession on the Delaware. This booklet (above) was published in 1656 to encourage more wealthy Dutchmen to settle in the colony.

In 1647, Peter Stuyvesant led his army into New Amsterdam to the cheers of Dutch settlers, portrayed in this English drawing (below). He became the governor of the colony, promising its inhabitants, "I shall rule you as a father his children." Within a month, he had ordered the village cleaned and the streets paved. But he also set strict rules about social conduct that the Dutch disliked.

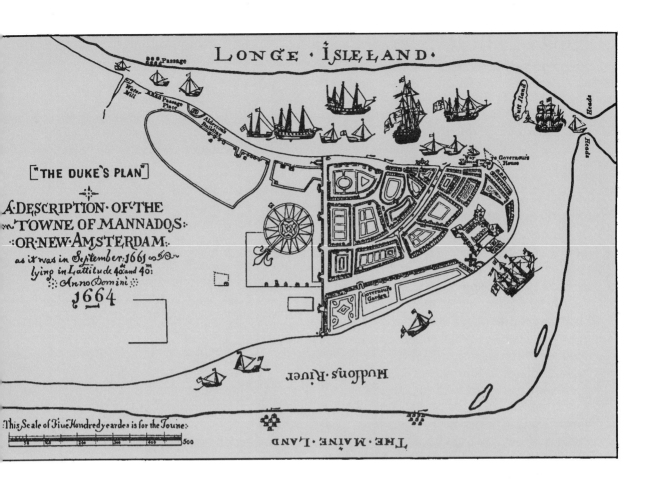

The town Peter Stuyvesant surrendered to the English was much different from what it was when he took it over fourteen years earlier. By 1664, more than a thousand people lived in New Amsterdam. They came from a variety of nationalities and spoke eighteen different languages. Many improvements in the town were also made. These included the building of the governor's house and gardens, which can be seen in this 1664 map of Manhattan (above).

"Never will I surrender," said Peter Stuyvesant to English officials at his farmhouse in August 1664. He refused to sign the Articles of Capitulation, which would have put New Amsterdam in the hands of the English. He changed his mind only when his advisers and his son Balthazar sent a personal request. His last words before surrendering the colony were, "I would [rather] have been carried to my grave." This nineteenth-century illustration (right) dramatically portrays his refusal to surrender to England.

KING PHILIP'S WAR

In 1661, King Massasoit died and his son, Alexander (also known as Wamsutta), became chief of the Wampanoag tribe. In 1664, Major Winslow of Plymouth forced Alexander to sell his land to the Plymouth colony. While being held by the colonists, Alexander died, and his brother Philip (also known as Metacomet) took over. Philip was upset at his tribe's increasing loss of power and angry at the settlers' purchase of Indian lands, hunting grounds, and fishing areas. In 1675, three of Philip's warriors were accused of the murder of John Sassamon, an Indian aide to Philip, who had been educated at Harvard. The English tried and killed the three Wampanoags, infuriating Philip. The incident sparked King Philip's War, one of the costliest wars in colonial history. On Sunday, June 20, 1675, Philip led the first attack of the war at Swansea, Massachusetts. Attacks continued throughout the next few months in the Plymouth and Massachusetts colonies, and in settlements on the Connecticut River. Much of the fighting was indecisive, because of poor leadership in the colonial army.

Like his father, Massasoit, Wampanoag leader King Philip (?-1676; also known as Metacomet) met with New England colonial leaders, portrayed in this illustration (opposite page, top) from a nineteenth-century textbook, to discuss Indian concerns peacefully. But as the number of settlers increased and Indian land grew smaller, he became angry. He told an English friend, "I am resolved not to see the day when I have no country."

To avenge the killing of three indians, King Philip began the bloodiest war in New England history. In 1695, he burned several Connecticut and Massachusetts frontier towns. To strengthen his attacks, Philip tried to unite several Massachusetts Indian tribes against the settlers. This map (opposite page, right) shows the towns where fighting took place.

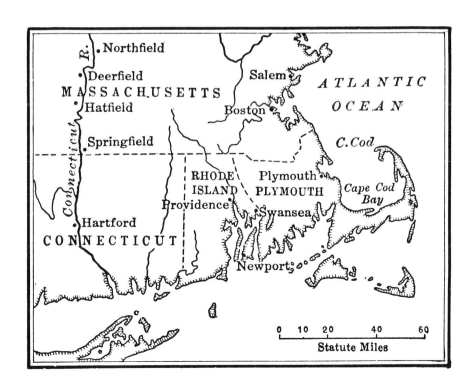

Captain Benjamin Church (1639-1718; left) was the military leader of the New England colonists during King Philip's War. A stout man of "uncommon activity," he was an able leader in a war led at times by incompetent men.

At dawn on May 10, 1676, over 150 men led by Captain William Turner, the figure with his arm upraised in this engraving (below), attacked the Indian settlement at Deerfield, near Hadley, Massachusetts. Several Indians were killed, some while sleeping in their tents, some in hand-to-hand combat, while others drowned in the Connecticut River. This attack was crucial in destroying the Indians' morale.

In the New World, colonists had to abandon their measured, predictable ways of fighting. They had to adapt to Indian ways of war, which were built on surprise and quick thinking. The colonists did have an advantage in terms of firearms, however. While not always accurate, these weapons often frightened the Indians with noise and smoke. This engraving (above) shows a confrontation between Indians and colonists in King Philip's War.

On February 9, 1676, Mary Rowlandson, of Massachusetts (c. 1635-78), was captured by the Wampanoags. For eleven weeks, she and her family traveled with the Indians. She won good treatment by her skills as a seamstress. She was returned to the colony for a payment of twenty English pounds. In 1682, she published The Sovereignty and Goodness of God (right). It was very popular in its time, and is now considered a revealing look at Indian life.

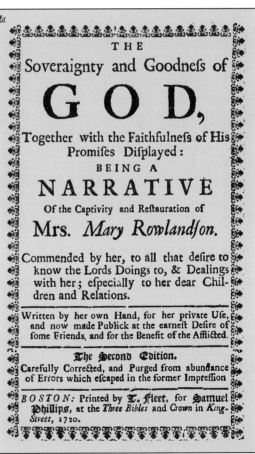

THE
Soveraignty and Goodneſs of
GOD,
Together with the Faithfulneſs of His Promiſes Diſplayed:
BEING A
NARRATIVE
Of the Captivity and Reſtauration of
Mrs. *Mary Rowlandſon.*

Commended by her, to all that deſire to know the Lords Doings to, & Dealings with her; eſpecially to her dear Children and Relations.

Written by her own Hand, for her private Uſe, and now made Publick at the earneſt Deſire of ſome Friends, and for the Benefit of the Afflicted.

The Second Edition.
Carefully Corrected, and Purged from abundance of Errors which eſcaped in the former Impreſſion

BOSTON: Printed by **T. Fleet,** for **Samuel Phillips,** at the *Three Bibles* and *Crown* in *King-Street,* 1720.

KING PHILIP'S WAR: THE CONCLUSION

In December 1675, Plymouth soldiers attacked the Narragansett tribe in Rhode Island. This began the Great Swamp Fight, which was the turning point in the war. It was a near-massacre: Hundreds of Indians were killed. Philip fled to Mohawk country in New York, in search of arms, rest, and allies. But he was rejected by the Mohawks and had to return to New England. In February, Philip and his warriors began a new offensive. They burned the town of Lancaster, Massachusetts, and attacked Plymouth Town and areas in the upper Connecticut Valley. These incidents were followed by destructive English attacks in Hadley, Massachusetts, and in Narragansett territory. Philip escaped to his home, near South Kingston, Rhode Island. He was hunted and killed in August 1676. Despite his death, fighting continued for another two years.

When the war finally ended, King Philip was gone and the Wampanoag tribe was crushed. But the price was nearly as high for the English. The colony nearly went bankrupt. Twelve towns were destroyed. One in every sixteen English men of military age died in battle—one thousand lives. Many settlers died of starvation. In proportion to population, King Philip's War took more lives than any war in American history.

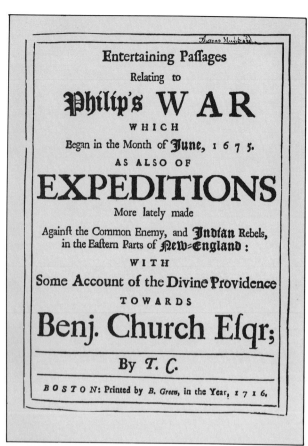

For months King Philip's War was a series of indecisive Indian raids and colonial retaliations. But the war moved in the colonists' favor with the Great Swamp Fight (opposite page, top). On December 11, 1675, thirteen hundred men from the Plymouth, Massachusetts Bay, and Rhode Island colonies practically destroyed the Narragansett tribe.

In 1716, the memoirs of Benjamin Church (above), the leader of the colonial forces in King Philip's War, were published. They were collected by Church's son, Thomas. He is the "T.C." named on the title page. The memoirs include accounts of Church's role in the war. In addition to leading troops to victory, he worked to convert Indians to Christianity, sometimes on the battlefield.

On August 12, 1676, death came to King Philip. Captain Church and his troops surrounded Philip's camp. An Indian friendly with the colonists shot Philip through the heart as he tried to escape. The event is rendered in this illustration from a nineteenth-century history book (left). Philip's head was displayed in the Plymouth blockhouse for several years. His wife Wootonekanuske and son were sold into slavery in Bermuda.

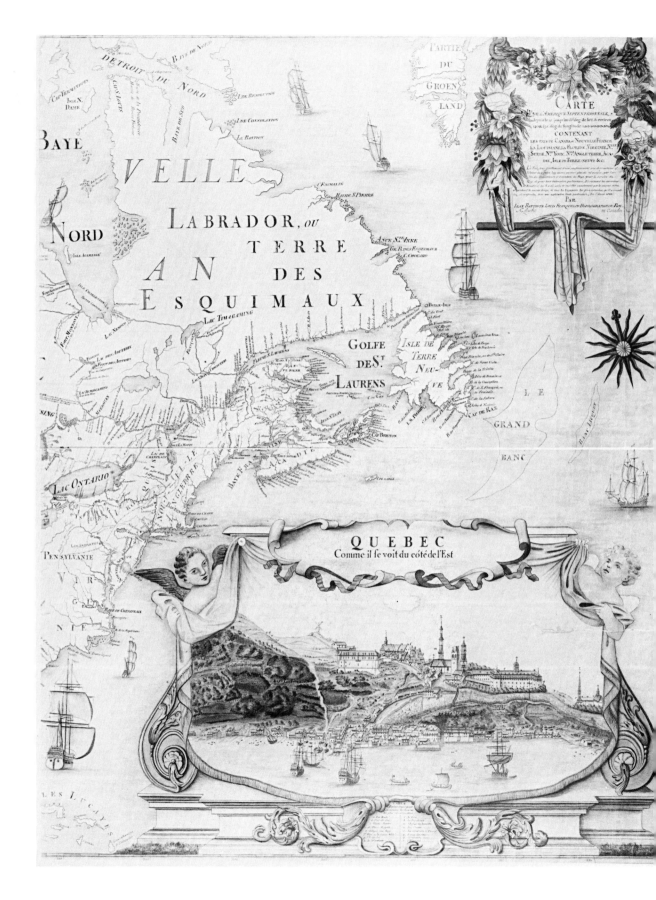

CAP TEEMUTICUS
ISLE N. DAME
BAYE DE NORD
DETROIT DU NORD
LOS JAUES
BAYE DES NO
I DE RESOLUTION
I DE CONSOLATION
LE BASTION
PARTIE DU GROEN LAND

BAYE

NORD

VELLE

LABRADOR, ou
TERRE
DES
ESQUIMAUX

ISLE AUAMISSE

AN

LAC TIMAGAMING

L'ESCHANTÉ
HAVRE S. PIERRE

ANCE S.te ANNE
Gr. BAYE ESQUIMAUX
C. CHOUARD

GOLFE
DE S.t
LAURENS

ISLE DE
TERRE
NEU
VE

BELLE-ISLE

LAC ONTARIO

PEN SYLVANIE

VIR
G
I
NIE

LES LUCAYES

NOUV. ANGLETERRE

LAC DE CHAMPLAIN

BAYE F. BA
A DI E

BAYE DE CHESAPEAK

RAYE DE CHESAPEAK

CAP BRETON

LE
GRAND
BANC

BANC BLANC LEQUET

CARTE
D'UNE L'AMERIQUE SEPTENTRIONALE,
Dressée sur Nouvelles Observations

CONTENANT
LES PAYS DE CANADA ou NOUVELLE FRANCE
LA LOUISIANE LA FLORIDE VIRGINIE N.lle
SUEDE N.lle YORC N.lle ANGLETERRE ACA-
DIE, ISLE DE TERRE-NEUVE &c.

PAR
JEAN BAPTISTE LOUIS FRANQUELIN HYDROGRAPHE DU ROY
EN CANADA

QUEBEC
Comme il se voit du côté de l'Est

Part II: 1677-1753
The Contests for North America

This map of New France was drawn by the French cartographer Jean Baptiste Louis Franquelin in 1688, two years before a small English fleet tried unsuccessfully to capture the city of Quebec. French artillery, positioned on the cliffs outside the city, drove back the English ships in May 1690.

Almost from the moment the first explorers reached its shores, North America became a theater in which the power plays of the European nations were acted out. By the last quarter of the seventeenth century, one of these European powers, England, had absorbed the colonies Sweden and Holland had planted in the decades before. England had also managed to restrict Spain's influence in eastern North America to its holdings in Florida.

As the 1680s ended, two great European empires—those of France and Britain—came into conflict. Over the next six decades, France and Britain would fight three major wars in North America. At stake was the control of a vast, rich continent. These wars were fought not only by English and French soldiers and settlers, but also by the land's original inhabitants—the Indians, who were forced to take sides in this conflict of colonial empires.

These three wars—King William's War (1689-97), Queen Anne's War (1701-13), and King George's War (1744-48)—saw battles in snowbound frontier settlements of New York, in the steaming swamps of Florida, and on the Atlantic islands that guarded the mouth of the St. Lawrence River, the gateway to New France. When they were over, Britain was firmly in control of the Atlantic seacoast from Florida to the St. Lawrence. But New France, stretching from Quebec to the Mississippi River Valley, remained a powerful force. It would take another, greater conflict—the French and Indian War of 1754-1763—to assure Britain's hold over North America east of the Mississippi.

A TIMELINE OF MAJOR EVENTS
PART II *1677-1753 The Contests for North America*

WORLD HISTORY

1678 Rumors of a "Popish Plot" to restore Catholicism in England lead to the persecution of Roman Catholics.

1679 France establishes the French African Company. Its aim is to export 2,000 slaves a year from Africa to the West Indies.

1685 Louis XIV of France revokes the Edict of Nantes, which had established tolerance for Protestants; renewed conflicts break out between France's Catholics and Protestants.

1687 Englishman Isaac Newton publishes one of the founding documents of modern science, *Philosophiae Naturalis Principia Mathematica* (The Mathematical Principles of Natural Philosophy). It contains

Isaac Newton

his theory of gravity.

1688 England's bloodless

"Glorious Revolution" overthrows Catholic king James II; he is replaced by his Dutch Protestant son-in-law William II, who rules jointly with Queen Mary.

1689 The English Parliament passes a Declaration of Rights, limiting the king's power and preventing Catholic rule.
•Peter the Great becomes czar of Russia and begins to modernize his nation.

COLONIAL HISTORY   BATTLES AND CONFLICTS

1677 Sir Edmund Andros builds a fort at Pemaquid, Maine, as a defense against Indian raids.

Sieur de La Salle

1678 King Philip's War ends when Edmund Andros makes peace with the Indians in Maine.

1680 French explorer Sieur de La Salle builds Fort Crèvecoeur on the Illinois River.

1684 La Salle and French colonists set out for Louisiana but are unable to find the mouth of the Mississippi River.

•New York governor Thomas Dongan signs a peace treaty with the Iroquois Indians.

1686 Port Royal, or Stuart Town, South Carolina, is destroyed by a Spanish force from Florida.

1689 Jacob Leisler leads a rebellion against the government in Albany. He seeks representative government in New York City.
•A combined French

and Indian force seizes the English fort at Pemaquid, Maine.
•Count Frontenac arrives from France to govern Canada. He plans to conquer the New England colonies, marking the start of King William's War between England and France.

1690 The Iroquois Indians renew their alliance with the English at Onondaga, New York.

COLONIAL HISTORY   GOVERNMENT

1678 England's Lords of Trade seek legal remedies against Massachusetts, which has

Seal of Pennsylvania

declared that English law does not "reach America."

1682 After traveling the Mississippi River for two years, René Robert Cavelier, sieur de La Salle, reaches its mouth. He claims all the land along the river's banks for France, and names the territory Louisiana.
•William Penn founds

Philadelphia and the Pennsylvania colony as a refuge for Quakers and other persecuted minorities.
•In Virginia, a 1670 law guaranteeing the freedom of Christian blacks arriving in America is repealed.

1683 Roger Williams, who founded Rhode Island as a haven for religious dissidents, dies.

1684 The High Court of Chancery in London repeals the Charter of Massachusetts, ending the Confederation of New England.

1689 Following the overthrow of King James II in England's "Glorious Revolution," New England colonies unseat the unpopular royal governor Edmund Andros and revert to their former separate governments.

1697 The Treaty of Ryswick ends the War of the Grand Alliance which began in 1689. The alliance was among England, Spain, Sweden, and the Holy Roman Empire against France, to counter the aggressions of Louis XIV.

1701 Disputes over who will rule Spain lead to the War of the Spanish Succession; England, Holland and several other states oppose France and Spain.

•Frederick of Brandenburg becomes Frederick I, first King of Prussia.

1702 King Charles II of Sweden captures the city of Warsaw, Poland, after leading his army to victory over an alliance of Poland, Russia and Denmark.

1704 Forces led by the Duke of Marlborough win a major victory over the forces of Spain and France at the Battle of Blenheim.

1707 England and Scotland are united as Great Britain.

Duke of Marlborough

1713 The Treaty of Utrecht ends the War of the Spanish Succession.
•The Russian czar Peter the Great builds a naval base at Tallin in Estonia.

1714 England's Queen Anne dies and is succeeded by a man who speaks no English: George I, Elector of Hanover and great-grandson of James I.

1702 The War of the Spanish Succession, known in the colonies as Queen Anne's War, begins.
•The British burn and loot St. Augustine, Florida, but are unable to capture the fort.

Street scene in St. Augustine

1704 French and Indian troops destroy Deerfield, Massachusetts.
•Carolina settlers and their Indian allies destroy Spanish missions in Appalachian territory.

1706 In Charleston, South Carolina, English settlers repulse a combined French and Spanish attack.

1707 Indians attack the English settlement at Winter Harbor, Maine.

1708 French and Indians massacre settlers at Haverhill, Massachusetts and capture the English settlement at St. John's, Newfoundland.

1711 A fleet of British warships sails from Boston to attack Quebec. The campaign is a disaster.
•The Tuscarora War between North and South Carolina settlers and the Tuscarora Indians begins.

1713 The Treaty of Utrecht ends Queen Anne's War, granting Britain Acadia (Nova Scotia), Hudson Bay, and Newfoundland and France Cape Breton Island and the St. Lawrence River islands.
•South Carolina forces capture the Tuscarora stronghold of Fort Nohucke, ending the war.

1698 Father Eusebio Francisco Kino leads a three-year expedition from Mexico to California, disproving the belief that California is an island.

1699 Brothers Pierre and Jacques Le Moyne establish Old Biloxi (present-day Ocean Springs, Mississippi), the first of several French settlements along the Gulf of Mexico.

1700 French settlers begin to construct forts, settlements, fur-trading posts, and Jesuit missions in the Illinois Territory.
•Boston orders all Roman Catholics to leave the city within three months.

1701 The Rev. John Pierpont, a Congregationalist, charters the Collegiate school at Saybrook, Connecticut. The school later

becomes Yale University.

French colonial cottage in Illinois

1702 Cotton Mather publishes his *Ecclesiastical History of*

New England.

1706 Anglicanism is adopted as the established religion of South Carolina. Quakers and Puritans resist.

1709 Quakers in Philadelphia found the first center for mental health care in the colonies.

1712 Pennsylvania bans the import of slaves.

A TIMELINE OF MAJOR EVENTS

PART II *1677-1753 The Contests for North America*

1716·1733

WORLD HISTORY

1717 France, Britain, and Holland form a Triple Alliance to curb Spanish ambitions. Philip V of Spain, Louis XIV's grandson, is claiming the French crown, and his wife, Elizabeth Farnese, wants her children to inherit family lands in Italy.
•Austrian troops drive the Turks out of Belgrade, ending Turkey's military ambitions in the Balkans.

1718 The Holy Roman Empire joins the Triple Alliance against Spain.
•Britain declares war on Spain.
•The Treaty of Passarowitz, between Emperor Charles V, the Venetians, and the Ottoman empire, ends the war with Turkey that began in 1714.

1726 Irish author Jonathan Swift's novel, *Travels into Several Remote Nations of the World*, popularly known as *Gulliver's Travels*, enjoys instant success.

1727 Spain and Britain go to war over Spain's seizure of Gibraltar.

1732 Frederick William I, king of Prussia, introduces compulsory military service and creates the fourth largest army in Europe after France, Austria, and Russia.

Frederick I of Prussia

COLONIAL HISTORY BATTLES AND CONFLICTS

1718 The dreaded pirate Edward Teach, known as Blackbeard, is killed in a sea battle off the Virginia coast.

1719 Natchez Indians capture Fort Rosalie, Mississippi, and kill or take captive most of the settlers there.

1727 When a year-long Anglo-Spanish War breaks out in Europe, English and Spanish settlers in the colonies use it as an excuse to attack each other.

1728 South Carolina English settlers destroy a Yamassee Indian village deep in Spanish territory near St. Augustine, Florida.

1729 A combined force of Chickasaw, Natchez, and Yazoo Indians attack French settlements in the

Natchez woman and child

Mississippi River Valley. These attacks limit French control of the region.

1730 French troops and their Choctaw Indian allies capture the chief of the Natchez Indians and enslave hundreds of Natchez women and children. However, many Natchez warriors escape the attack.

COLONIAL HISTORY GOVERNMENT

1716 Virginia governor Alexander Spotswood leads an expedition across the Blue Ridge Mountains into the Shenandoah Valley, spurring westward expansion.

1718 On behalf of the French Company of the West, Baptiste Le Moyne, sieur de Bienville, founds New Orleans at the mouth of the Mississippi. In 1722, the city becomes capital of the Louisiana Territory.

Oglethorpe's book encouraging settlement in Georgia

1720 The French Treasury is bankrupted by the failure of the Mississippi Company, which has sponsored a financially disastrous settlement plan known as the Mississippi Bubble.

1722 The Six Nations of the Iroquois Confederation (Mohawk, Oneida, Onondaga, Cayuga, Seneca, and Tuscarora) make a treaty with the Virginia colonists agreeing not to cross the Potomac River or move west of the Blue Ridge Mountains.

1733 James Edward Oglethorpe founds Savannah and the colony of Georgia, the last of the original thirteen colonies, as a haven for the poor and as a buffer against Spanish and French colonies in the southeast.

1737 Austria, in alliance with Russia, declares war on the Ottoman (Turkish) empire.
•Swedish botanist Carl von Linne, also known as Linnaeus, publishes his *Genera Plantarum*, introducing an important new way of classifying plants and animals.

1739 Frederick II, "the Great," becomes king of Prussia.

1740 The War of the Austrian Succession

begins; in America it is called King George's War.

1742 Indian slaves in Peru, lead by Juan Santos, rebel against their Spanish masters and defeat them in several battles.

1745 Charles Edward Stuart ("Bonnie Prince Charlie") lands in Scotland in an attempt to restore Britain to Stuart rule.

Charles Edward Stuart

1748 The ruins of the ancient city of Pompeii, buried by an eruption of the volcano Vesuvius in AD 79, are discovered near Naples, Italy.

1749 Bonnie Prince Charlie's supporters, called Jacobites, are defeated at the Battle of Culloden Moor in Scotland.

1750 Johann Sebastian Bach, the great composer, dies in Leipzig, Germany.

1739 Britain declares war on Spain, beginning the War of Jenkin's Ear. Officially, the war is on behalf of an English sea captain whose ear was cut off by Spanish coastguards in the West Indies.

1740 With the aid of the Cherokee, Chickasaw, and Creek Indians, Georgia leader James Oglethorpe invades Spanish Florida. His forces are repelled at St. Augustine, Florida.

1743 Oglethorpe attacks Spanish settlements around St. Augustine, again in retaliation for Spanish raids on Georgia settlements.

James Edward Oglethorpe

1744 France joins Spain in the war against England, beginning what is called King George's War in the colonies.

1745 A New England force attacks and finally captures the important French fort Louisbourg on Cape Breton Island, which guards the approach to the St. Lawrence River.
•French forces attack Albany and burn the settlement at Saratoga

in New York. These attacks are in revenge for raids by England's Iroquois allies.

1748 The Treaty of Aix-la-Chapelle ends King George's War.

1752 Virginia signs the Treaty of Logstown with the Delaware and Iroquois Indians. In return the Indians cede the land south of the Ohio River to the Ohio Company.

1735 General James Oglethorpe invites a group of Moravian Protestants to settle in Georgia.

1739 Preacher George Whitefield sparks a religious revival in the northern colonies.
•In a South Carolina

slave rebellion, twenty-one whites and forty-four blacks are killed.

1741 Moravian settlers arrive in Bethlehem, Pennsylvania.

1747 Virginia settlers and Pennsylvania traders move into the Ohio Territory on land granted to the Ohio Company, prompting French settlers in the area to construct a line of forts across western Pennsylvania.

1749 Inspired by Benjamin Franklin, Philadelphia founds an institution of higher learning, the forerunner of the University of Pennsylvania.

1750 German craftspeople in Pennsylvania develop the Conestoga wagon, soon to become the frontier's standard vehicle.

Moravian settlers

KING WILLIAM'S WAR

King William's War (1689-97) was the first of four conflicts between England and France for control of North America. In the 1680s, King Louis XIV of France tried to conquer neighboring European lands. England, the Netherlands, Austria, and other nations joined together to try to stop him. In Europe, the war was called the War of the Grand Alliance. In America, it was called King William's War, after England's King William III.

Fighting began in 1689, when the Iroquois Indians, allies of the English, attacked the Canadian village of La Chine. The French struck back in February 1690, with an attack on the New York village of Schenectady. During the next few years, the French and their Indian allies raided frontier settlements in New Hampshire and Maine. In May 1690, a small New England fleet led by Sir William Phips captured Port Royal on the island of Acadia (now Nova Scotia). Later that year, Phips tried to capture Quebec, but his fleet was turned back by French artillery. A planned English land attack on Montreal fell apart because of poor organization.

In 1697, the Treaty of Ryswick ended the European war between France and the alliance of England, Spain, and the Netherlands. Little had been accomplished in the colonies, except to intensify the struggle between the French and the English for land, trade, and the Indians' loyalties. Sporadic fighting continued in America.

King William III (1650-1702; above) was not born in England. He was the prince of the Dutch state of Orange and, from 1672, ruler of the Netherlands. William was married to Mary (1662-94), daughter of King James II (1633-1701) of England. In the "Glorious Revolution" of 1688, rebels in England replaced James II with William and Mary, who ruled jointly. William brought England into war with France.

This French map (opposite page, top) shows the British attack on Quebec in 1690 during King William's War. Sir William Phips's fleet of thirty-four ships (Vaisseaux Anglois, "English vessels") floats in the St. Lawrence River. Up to two thousand colonial troops storm the lowlands near the city (dessente des Anglois, "descent of the English").

Sir William Phips (1651-95) made his fortune with ships like these (opposite page, bottom)— first as a ship's carpenter, then as a ship-builder and trader. His nautical experience was vital during King William's War.

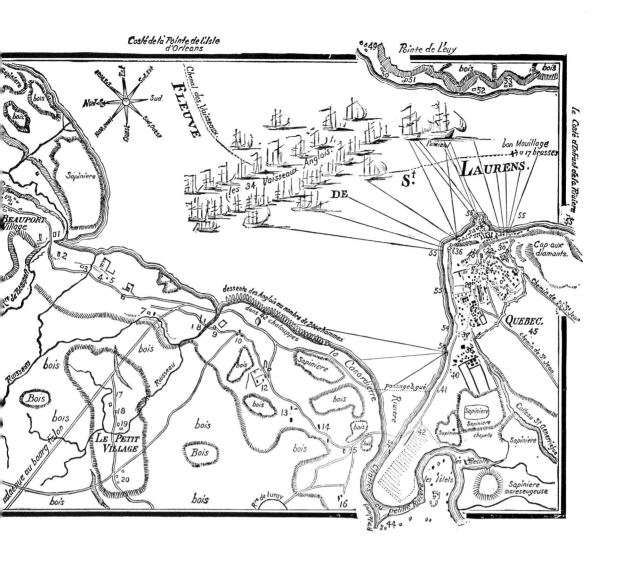

QUEEN ANNE'S WAR

In 1701, war in Europe broke out again. Against the wishes of other leaders, King Louis XIV of France had placed one of his grandsons on the throne of Spain. England, the Netherlands, and other countries declared war on France and Spain. In Europe it was called the War of the Spanish Succession. In America it was called Queen Anne's War (1701-13), after the reigning queen of England.

The frontiers of New England again suffered French and Indian raids. The most famous raid took place in Deerfield, Massachusetts, in 1704. In 1710, English colonial troops captured Port Royal in Acadia, as they had in the last war. This time they kept it, renaming it "Annapolis" in honor of Queen Anne. In the South, troops from the English colony of South Carolina burned the Spanish town of Pensacola in Florida in 1707.

In 1711, the English again tried and failed to capture Quebec. A fleet of seventy ships from England got no closer than the Gulf of St. Lawrence, where several ships were wrecked in bad weather. However, England won victories in Europe and at sea that forced France to make peace. In 1713, the Peace of Utrecht ended Queen Anne's War. England won Acadia (renamed Nova Scotia) and gained expanded trading rights in Spanish America.

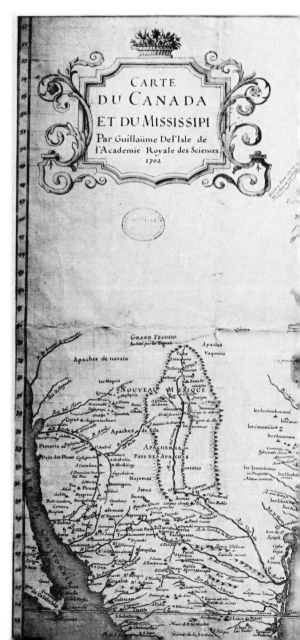

Queen Anne (1665-1714; opposite page) was the younger sister of Mary II. She came to the throne in 1702. A mild-mannered, conservative woman, she reigned over a time of war. But hers was also a reign of great literary and political achievement. English writers of the time included Jonathan Swift and the poet Alexander Pope. Scotland and England were united to form Great Britain in 1707.

This French map (below) shows the European colonies in North America at the beginning of Queen Anne's War. Most of the fighting took place on the frontiers of Nouvelle Angleterre (New England) and in Acadie (Acadia).

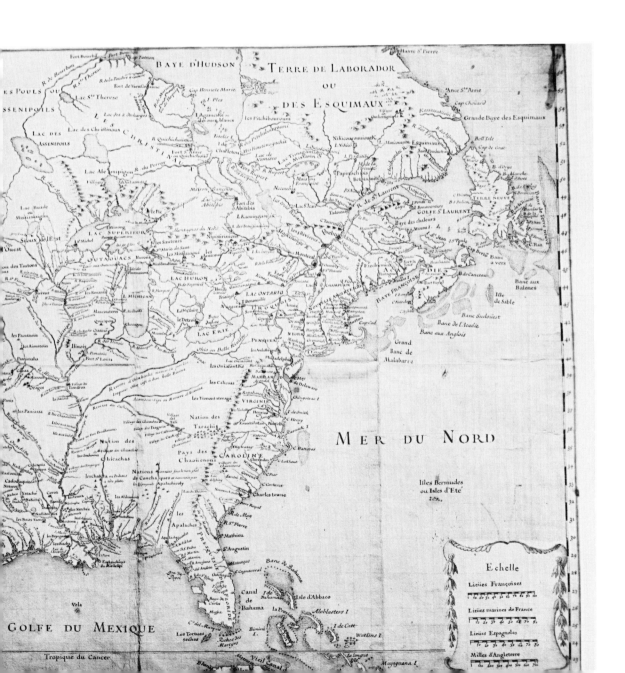

The most famous raid of Queen Anne's War was the attack on Deerfield, Massachusetts. Deerfield had about three hundred people and forty-one houses like this one (left). Early on February 29, 1704, a band of about fifty French soldiers and two hundred Abenaki and Caughnawaga Indians attacked the sleeping village. About fifty settlers were killed and a hundred taken prisoner. Nearly half the houses were burned.

THE
HISTORY
OF THE
Wars of *New-England*,
With the *Eaſtern* Indians.
OR, A
NARRATIVE
Of their continued Perfidy and Cruelty,
from the 10th of *Auguſt*, 1703.
To the Peace renewed 13th of *July*, 1713.
And from the 25th of *July*, 1722.
To their Submiſſion 15th *December*, 1725.
Which was Ratified *Auguſt* 5th 1726.

By *Samuel Penhallow*, Eſqr.

Neſcio tu quibus es, Lector, lecturus Ocellis,
Hoc ſcio, quod ſiccis, ſcribere non potui.

BOSTON:
Printed bv *T. Fleet*, for *S. Gerriſh* at the lower
end of *Cornbill*, and *D. Henchman* over-againſt
the Brick Meeting-Houſe in *Cornbill*, 1726.

This nineteenth-century woodcut (opposite page, bottom) shows
Indians leaving Deerfield with two prisoners. Indians often
attacked at night while their victims slept. Unlike European
armies, they were not afraid to attack in winter, when the snow
muffled their footsteps and pursuit by the enemy was difficult.

Stories of Indian wars made exciting reading for colonists. Samuel
Penhallow's book (above, right), published in Boston in 1726,
describes Indian battles during and after Queen Anne's War.

To protect their houses from attack, English colonists built fortifications like these (above, left).

COLONISTS AND INDIANS CLASH IN THE SOUTHEAST

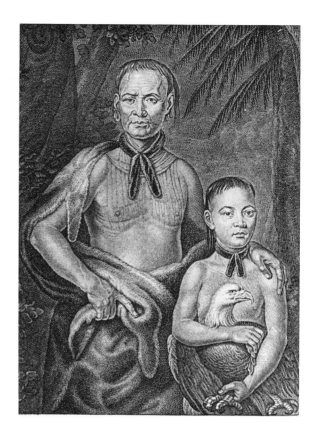

In the South as in the North, relations between English colonists and Indians were usually poor. Near the end of Queen Anne's War, tensions in North Carolina erupted in the Tuscarora War (1711-13). British settlers there had begun to crowd out the Tuscarora tribe. Some colonists kidnapped Tuscarora children to sell into slavery. The tribe asked the governor of Pennsylvania to allow them to move to that colony, but the request was refused. In September 1711, the Tuscaroras went to war. They killed dozens of settlers and nearly destroyed the settlement of New Bern. South Carolina sent troops, along with Cherokee Indians allied with the colonists, to help the settlers of North Carolina. In March 1713, the Tuscaroras were forced to make peace. The tribe moved to New York and became the sixth nation of the Iroquois Confederacy.

In 1715, fighting broke out in South Carolina between the colonists and the Yamasee tribe, who were angry about trade abuses and the loss of their land. Other tribes joined them. Troops from neighboring colonies had to be brought in before the uprising could be stopped in 1716.

Not all Indian-colonial relations were hostile. The powerful Creek Confederacy favored English traders and granted land to the new English colony of Georgia in 1732. After first helping the Yamasee in their uprising, the Creek tried to stay neutral in war.

Tomochichi (above) was the leader of Yamacraw, a Creek-Yamasee town near Savannah, Georgia. He welcomed James Oglethorpe (1696-1785), founder of Georgia. In 1734, he invited missionaries to set up Christian schools for his people. The schools lasted from about 1735 to 1739.

In this engraving (opposite page, bottom) Tuscarora Indians hunt the North Carolina woods for colonists. Two colonists hide in the brush. The Indians walk single file, their favored method for traveling through the forest.

This rough map of South Carolina (opposite page, top) was first drawn on a deerskin by an Indian chief about 1730. On the left is Charleston ("Charlestown"). To the west and northwest are lands inhabited by Indian tribes.

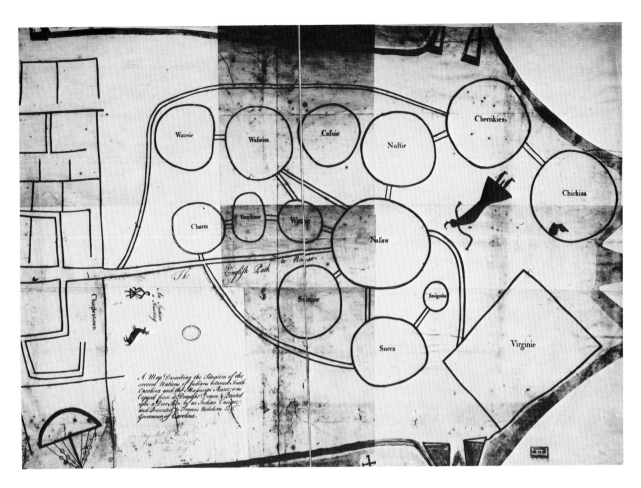

A Map Describing the Situation of the
several Nations of Indians between South
Carolina and the Massisipi River; was
Copyed from a Draught Drawn & painted
upon a Deer Skin by an Indian Cacique;
and Presented to Francis Nicholson Esq.
Governour of Carolina.

DIPLOMACY AND BLOODSHED IN THE MISSISSIPPI VALLEY

In the late 1600s, the French opened a new frontier: the Mississippi River valley. The French set up forts and fur-trading posts along the river. They made alliances with Indian groups such as the Illinois Confederacy of what is now Illinois. But the Fox tribe, enemies of the Illinois, wanted to keep control of the fur trade in their own hands. The Fox fought the French from 1712 to 1718. In 1728, the Fox, this time with the Sauk, began raiding French outposts again. During the war, the French destroyed many Fox and Sauk villages in what is now Wisconsin. In 1740, peace was made.

Meanwhile, in the French province of Louisiana in the South, war broke out with the Natchez tribe of what is now Mississippi. The Natchez worshiped the sun and had a royal family they believed was divine. They resented the high-handed ways of the French and the invasion of their land. On November 28, 1729, the Natchez went to war. With other tribes, such as the Yazoo, they killed hundreds of French settlers and traders. But by 1730, the French and their allies, the Choctaw, had nearly wiped out the Natchez. About four hundred Natchez prisoners were sold into slavery. Some Natchez fled to join the Chickasaw, Creek, and Cherokee tribes, all friendly to the English.

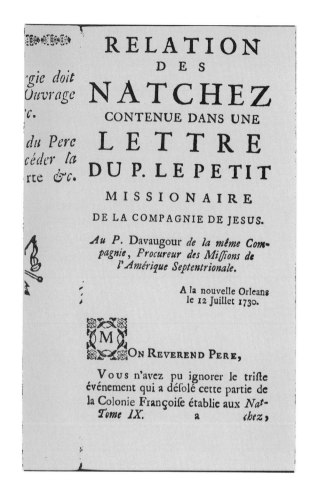

The violence of the Natchez uprising chilled the hearts of French people who heard of it. This version of the story is based on an eyewitness account told by a Jesuit missionary in a letter to P. Davaugour, his superior (above).

In the late 1600s, the Illinois Confederacy welcomed the arrival of French explorer and trader René Robert Cavelier, Sieur de La Salle (1643-87). The Illinois needed defenders against their enemies. In this eighteenth-century engraving (opposite page, top), Illinois Indians present the calumet, or peace pipe, to a French trader.

The French Fort St. Pierre (right) was built on the Yazoo River, in what is now Mississippi, in 1718. During the Natchez War, it was destroyed by the Koroa and Yazoo Indians.

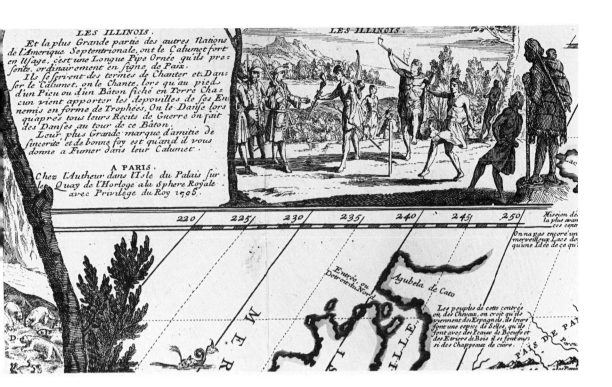

LES ILLINOIS.

Et la plus Grande partie des autres Nations de l'Amerique Septentrionale, ont le Calumet fort en Usage, c'est une Longue Pipe Ornée qu'ils presentent, ordinairement en signe de Paix.

Ils se servent des termes de Chanter et Danser le Calumet, on le Chante, lors qu'au pied d'un Pieu ou d'un Bâton fiché en Terre Chacun vient apporter les depouilles de ses Ennemis en forme de Trophées, On le Danse lors quapres tous leurs Recits de Guerre on fait des Danses au tour de ce Bâton.

Leur plus Grande marque d'amitie de sincerité et de bonne foy est qu'and il vous donne a Fumer dans leur Calumet.

A PARIS.

Chez l'Autheur dans l'Isle du Palais sur le Quay de l'Horloge a la Sphere Royale. avec Privilege du Roy 1705.

LES ILLINOIS.

220 / 225 / 230 / 235 / 240 / 245 / 250

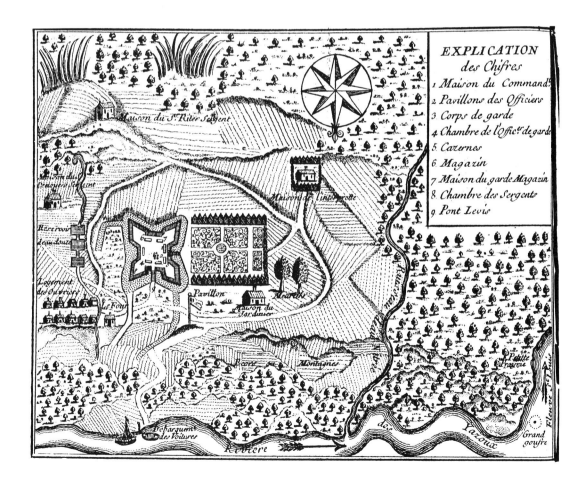

JAMES OGLETHORPE ATTACKS THE SPANISH IN FLORIDA

In the 1730s, British ships traded in South America and the West Indies in violation of treaties protecting Spanish merchants. A British captain named Robert Jenkins claimed that the Spanish had cut off his ear to punish him for smuggling. In October 1739, the War of Jenkins' Ear broke out between Britain and Spain—partly to avenge the injury to Jenkins but mainly to extend British power. As the war opened, Spain captured a British fort on Amelia Island at the disputed border between Florida and Georgia. General James Oglethorpe, governor of Georgia, responded with an attack on Florida. His army captured two Spanish forts on the St. Johns River. In 1740, Oglethorpe laid siege to the old Florida town and fortress of St. Augustine. But the defenders were too powerful, and Oglethorpe retreated. In 1742, the Spanish won a victory at St. Simon's Island, off the Georgia coast, but were later defeated at the Battle of Bloody Marsh. Battles also took place elsewhere in the New World. Three thousand colonial volunteers took part in a failed British attack on Cartagena in South America in 1740. In 1744, the war with Spain merged with King George's War.

General James Edward Oglethorpe (above) founded the colony of Georgia in 1732 as a home for imprisoned debtors and other needy people. The colony, Oglethorpe knew, would also serve as a defense against the Spanish in Florida and the French in Louisiana. During the War of Jenkins' Ear, Oglethorpe led Georgia troops against the Spanish.

ing yourself on all Occasions, in Support and
fence of the real Interest and Glory of our
and Country, the Liberties and Com-
e of the Nation, the Independence of
ments, and particularly the Privileges of
y; and are highly sensible, how much
tend to our Happiness, and our Pos-
have Men of such Sentiments as
in every Station attended with
uence.

eceived with the utmost good
race took Care to warm
blest Sentiments of Duty
their Country.

, 18.

Winter Gally, Capt.
Gibraltar, was
, and car-
Capt.

under his Command, from *Torbay*, where he
had continued about a Month, wind-bound.

SATURDAY, 23.

There were Advices from *Carolina*, that
Gen. *Oglethorpe* had made himself Master of
some of the Out-works of St. *Augustine*,
that thereupon the Garison retir'd into the
Citadel, and that it was not at all doubted,
he would be soon Master of the Place. Tho'
afterwards we had an Account, that a De-
tachment from the Garison had kill'd and
wounded several of his Men.

MONDAY, 25.

Vice-Admiral *Balchen*, and Capt. *Anson*,
with their Squadrons, Transports, &c. the
Wind coming contrary, return'd to St. *Helen's*.

At the Assizes at *Chelmsford*, 11 Persons
were capitally convicted, three of whom, *viz.*
two Brothers, and the Daughter of one of

---

*People in England were hungry for news of the war with Spain.
This issue of* The Monthly Chronologer *(above), a London newspaper, reports "advices from Carolina" about General Oglethorpe's
siege of St. Augustine in 1740. News traveled far more slowly in
those days than it does now. The report was filed Saturday,
August 23—several months after the siege began.*

*This map (below) shows Oglethorpe's attack on St. Augustine,
Florida, in 1740. The town and fort (upper right) are besieged by
English ships. In June, after thirty-eight days, Oglethorpe was
forced to retreat.*

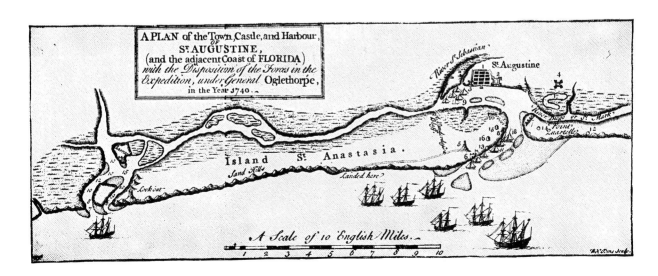

KING GEORGE'S WAR

As Britain's war with Spain continued, its long peace with France weakened. Britain and France took opposite sides in the War of Austrian Succession, which began in 1740. Britain supported Austria, and France supported Prussia. In 1744, Britain and France openly declared war on each other. King George's War (1744-48), named for England's King George II, had begun.

The French captured Canso in British Nova Scotia in 1744. The British set their sights on Louisbourg, a mighty French fortress on Cape Breton Island that was thought to be nearly impossible to conquer. It protected the Gulf of St. Lawrence from invasion. William Pepperell, leading a force of about four thousand New England soldiers, decided to try. Aided by warships from England, Pepperell's men laid siege to Louisbourg from April 30 to June 15, 1745. Under a constant barrage of artillery fire, Louisbourg surrendered.

Most of the other fighting in King George's War took the form of bloody raids by both sides on the frontiers of New York and New England. In 1748, the Peace of Aix-la-Chapelle ended the war. Many English colonists were outraged when Louisbourg, in an exchange of territories, was returned to France.

King George II (1683-1760; above) came to the English throne in 1727 and gave his name to the war in America. Like his father, George I (1660-1727), he was a German prince distantly related to Queen Anne. Neither king ever learned to speak English well or had much interest in government. They left policy to their advisers.

William Pepperell (1696-1759; right) was the commander of the New England land forces that attacked Louisbourg in 1745. Born in what is now Maine, he became very rich through lumbering, shipbuilding, and trading. Pepperell served on the Massachusetts Provincial Council and in other government posts. For his service at Louisbourg, he was made a baronet (nobleman).

The fortified town of Louisbourg was built on the east coast of Cape Breton Island. It guarded the mouth of the Gulf of St. Lawrence and sheltered French traders and privateers (merchant ships authorized to attack enemy vessels). This picture (below) shows Louisbourg during the siege of 1745.

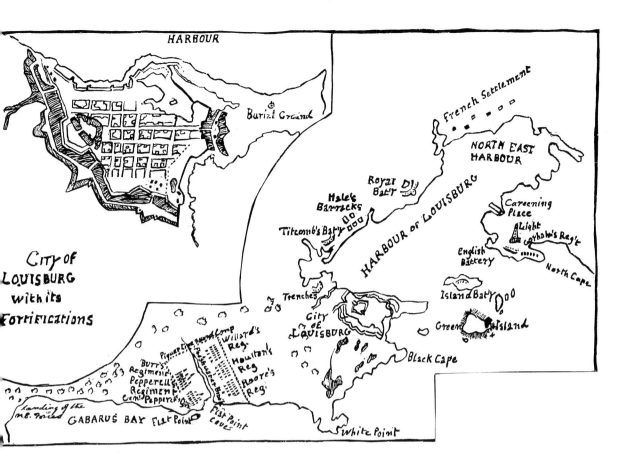

This map (above) shows Pepperell's plan for besieging Louisbourg. The colonial army landed at Gabarus Bay and set up camp at Flat Point, three miles west of the city. Cannons were dragged to the hills behind the city. The French Royal Battery ("Royal Bat'y") was captured, as was Lighthouse Point east of the city. In time, a ring of cannons bombarded Louisbourg.

The four thousand men who captured Louisbourg were mostly "citizen soldiers"—ordinary farmers and fishermen with little experience of war. They had to learn the basics of military art. This manual (opposite page, top) shows infantrymen how to load and fire a musket.

Pepperell rides triumphantly among his troops after the surrender of Louisbourg on June 15, 1745 (opposite page, bottom).

Part III: 1754-1763
The French and Indian War

British general James Wolfe (1727-59) led the most important campaign of the French and Indian War: the assault on the Canadian capital of Quebec in 1759. Wolfe was only thirty-two at the time. Thin, red-haired, and sickly, Wolfe was a brave soldier and a learned student of war. His boldness and cunning in directing battles were second to none.

The last great conflict waged between European powers in North America was the French and Indian War, which lasted from 1754 to 1763. Before the war, Britain controlled northern Canada and the eastern seaboard from Newfoundland to Georgia as far west as the western edge of the Appalachian Mountains. The French controlled, though less surely, the much larger tracts of land known as New France and Louisiana, which stretched from the Gulf of St. Lawrence to the Gulf of Mexico and the Rocky Mountains, and included the Great Lakes and the Ohio, Mississippi, and Missouri river systems. Florida and the southwest were still Spanish, and the Pacific northwest was still largely unexplored.

In 1763, the Treaty of Paris brought the French and Indian War to an end, with France abandoning its North American claims between the Mississippi and the Appalachians. According to the Treaty, these formerly French lands were to be reserved for the Indians, and white settlement in them was forbidden.

This provision of the treaty was promptly ignored. Britain now controlled Canada east of the Rockies and America east of the Mississippi, so British traders and settlers quickly took advantage of the fact. France and Spain still controlled Louisiana and New Spain, which stretched from the Mississippi to the Pacific and Mexico, while in the northwest, Spain and Russia were quarreling over the Oregon territory. But Britain was now the overwhelming force in North America, and the domains which the Revolutionary War would later create as the United States were firmly established.

A TIMELINE OF MAJOR EVENTS

PART III *1754-1763 The French and Indian War*

1754-1758

WORLD HISTORY

1755 An earthquake devastates Portugal's capital, Lisbon, killing at least 10,000 people and destroying three-quarters of the city.
•Dr. Samuel Johnson publishes his *Dictionary of the English Language.*

1756 Frederick II of Prussia invades Saxony after learning of an agreement between six European states, including France and Russia,

to divide Prussia between them. The Seven Years War begins.
•Britain forms an alliance with Prussia and declares war on France.
•France and Austria sign a treaty of alliance.
•William Pitt the Elder becomes Britain's Prime Minister and takes charge of the war against France.

1757 Robert Clive

William Pitt the Elder

retakes Calcutta from the French, and defeats a much larger Bengali army at the battle of Plassey, thus assuring the British East India Company's rule over most of India.
•**November 5** Prussian troops, led by Frederick II, defeat French and Austrian forces at the battle of Rossbach.

June 23,1758 A British and Hanoverian army defeats the French at Krefeld.

COLONIAL HISTORY **BATTLES AND CONFLICTS**

1754 In the opening battle of the French and Indian War, George Washington leads 150 Virginians to victory over French settlers in the Ohio River Valley.
•Washington builds Fort Necessity at Great Meadows, Pennsylvania, and repulses a large French force led by Coulon de Villiers.

1755 British general Edward Braddock's

troops are ambushed by French and Indians near Fort Duquesne (Pittsburgh) in the Battle of the Wilderness. Braddock is killed; George Washington assumes command of the army.
•In the Battle of Lake George, colonial and British forces defeat 1,400 French and Indians.

1756 French troops

under the Marquis de Montcalm destroy the British forts at Oswego and Lake George in New York.

1757 Fort William Henry, on Lake George, surrenders to Montcalm, but is then attacked by Indians. Some 1,400 survivors reach safety at Fort Edward, New York.

1758 General James Abercrombie attacks the French at Fort

Fort William Henry

Ticonderoga, New York, with 15,000 soldiers. French commander Montcalm, with 3,000 men, repels them.

COLONIAL HISTORY **GOVERNMENT**

1754 Meeting at Albany, New York, delegates from seven northern colonies approve Benjamin Franklin's proposal for a union of the colonies. The plan is later rejected by the colonial legislatures.
•King's College (later Columbia University) is founded in New York City. Clergyman Samuel Johnson is its first president.

1755 Britain banishes defeated French colonists from Acadia. Some travel to Louisiana, where they settle and become known as Acadians, or Cajuns.

1757 Benjamin Franklin is sent to London as the agent of the Pennsylvania Assembly.

1758 Puritan theologian Jonathan Edwards is

The exile of the Acadians

appointed president of the College of New Jersey, but dies shortly after taking office. The Rev. Aaron Burr is named as the college's second president.
•Slave traders are

barred from the annual meeting of the Society of Friends (Quakers) in Philadelphia.
•Touro Synagogue, serving the Jewish congregation in Newport Rhode Island, is built.

1759 August 1 British and Hanoverian troops defeat the French at the Battle of Minden.
August 12 Austrian and Russian forces inflict a major defeat on the Prussians at Kunersdorf.

1760 George III becomes king of Great Britain following the death of his grandfather, King George II.
October 9 Russian and Austrian troops enter Berlin.

•British troops led by Eyre Coote win a decisive victory over the French at Wandiwash in southern India. French hopes of an Indian empire are crushed.

1761 Catherine II becomes czarina of Russia.
•Spain enters the Seven Years War on the side of the French coalition.
•British troops recapture Pondicherry, India, from the French.

1762 Britain declares war on Spain and captures many of Spain's Caribbean colonies, as well as the Philippines in the Pacific.
•Prussia and Sweden sign a peace treaty.
July 21 Prussia defeats Austria at the battle of Berkersdorf in Silesia.
November 24 Austria and Prussia sign a truce.

1763 The Treaty of Paris ends the Seven Years War. Britain wins a great victory from the

conflict.
•To help pay off its war debt, the British Parliament passes the Sugar Act, taxing the American colonies.
August 25 A Russian army invades Prussia, and is defeated at the battle of Zorndorf.

1759 June General James Wolfe advances up the St. Lawrence River with a force of 9,000 men in a fleet commanded by Admiral Charles Saunders.
July The French fort Niagara falls to a British force of 2,000 and 100 Iroquois Indians.
•The French blow up Fort Carillon at Ticonderoga, New York, to avoid its capture by the British; the French also abandon Fort St. Frederick, New York.

September British troops attack Quebec. Generals Montcalm and Wolfe are both killed, and Quebec surrenders.

General James Wolfe

1760 Cherokee Indians attack Fort Prince George, South Carolina, in an unsuccessful effort to rescue hostages.
•The French outpost at Detroit, Michigan, surrenders to the British.

1761 The Cherokees seek peace and end raids on frontier settlements.

1762 France cedes its land west of the Mississippi River, the region known as Upper

Louisiana, to Spain.

1763 The Treaty of Paris formally ends the French and Indian War. France gives up Nova Scotia, Cape Breton Island, and the St. Lawrence River islands to the British.
•Ottawa chief Pontiac declares war on British garrisons around the Great Lakes; Indian forces capture forts Sandusky (Ohio) and Michillimackinac (Michigan).

•Michael Hillegas of Philadelphia opens America's first music store.
•The colonies' first life insurance company, the Presbyterian Ministers Fund, is organized in Philadelphia.

1760 Students at the College of William and Mary in Williamsburg, Virginia, protest poor food in an early case of campus unrest.
•Daniel Boone is commissioned to scout the

frontier in the region of present-day eastern Tennessee.

1761 New Hampshire gets its first public transport when Englishman John Stavers opens a stagecoach line between Portsmouth and Boston.
•Boston lawyer James Otis challenges the legality of writs permitting British customs officials to search private property.

1762 The Protestant Moravian community in Bethlehem, Pennsylvania, abandons its twenty-one year experiment in communal living.
•John Bartram, appointed Botanist Royal, studies the plant life of Florida.

1763 In an effort to reduce the cost of defending frontier settlements against Indian attacks, the British government bans settle-

ment west of the Appalachian Mountains.

A John Bartram illustration

THE BATTLE OF THE WILDERNESS

The first shots of the French and Indian War were fired in 1754 at Great Meadows in what is now western Pennsylvania. There, British and French troops fought over possession of the Ohio River Valley. The valley was prized for its fertile land, waterways, and fur trade. To protect their claim, the French had built Fort Duquesne in the valley, at the site of present-day Pittsburgh. In 1754, the British colony of Virginia sent an army to attack the fort. The French defeated the Virginians at Fort Necessity in the Battle of Great Meadows on July 4.

The following year, General Edward Braddock arrived from England to avenge the defeat. On June 10, 1755, with an army of about two thousand troops, Braddock set out from Virginia. Progress through the mountainous wilderness was much slower than he expected. He was forced to split his army in two—an advance column of about fourteen hundred men, the rest following more slowly. On July 9, 1755, less than ten miles from Fort Duquesne, the advance column met the enemy. An army of about eight hundred French, Canadians, and Indians hid behind trees and fired into the British column. Because Braddock knew only European warfare, which took place on open battlefields, he refused to let his men take cover. Nearly a thousand British were killed or wounded. The survivors fled. The battle became known as the Battle of the Wilderness, or Braddock's Defeat.

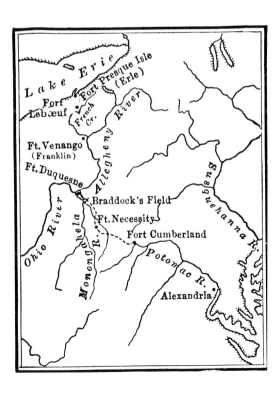

George Washington (1732-99; above, right) was twenty-two when war with the French broke out. In 1754, he led about four hundred troops that were defeated by twice as many French forces at Great Meadows in what is now Pennsylvania. In 1755 he served as an aide to General Braddock in the Ohio River Valley.

Washington's expense account (above, left) claims refunds for the money he spent on "Cleaning my Pistols," "Milk," and "Washing."

It took Braddock's army nearly a month to march the roughly one hundred miles indicated by the dotted line on this map (right, below). Braddock had hoped it would take four days.

General Edward Braddock (1695–1755; left) was no stranger to battle. A short, fat, hot-tempered man, he disciplined his troops strictly. He had fought bravely in Europe, but he had no understanding of how different warfare in America was. He told colonial leader Benjamin Franklin: "Upon the king's regular and disciplined troops, sir, it is impossible they [the Indians] should make any impression."

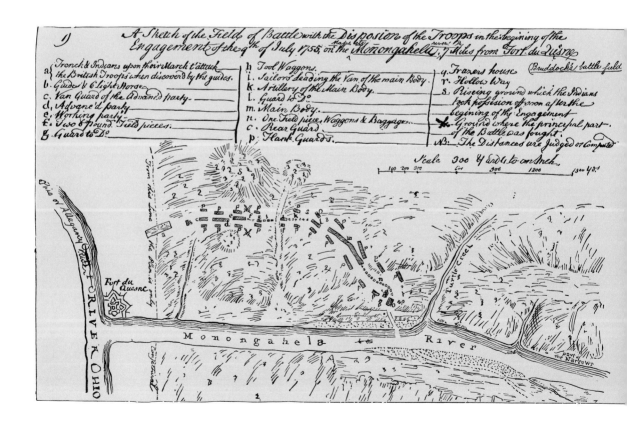

The wilderness of the Allegheny Mountains had no roads when Braddock marched across it. Slowly and painfully, Braddock's men cleared a path by cutting trees and blasting rock. In this illustration (above), a band beating drums marches at the head of the column. In the distance is the wagon train, carrying supplies.

In rough, sketchy language, this map (left) tells the story of an afternoon of horror. The line of shaded rectangles represents Braddock's advance column. The French and Indians came out of Fort Duquesne at left. During the battle, the Indians captured a hill (the circular area marked "S" at the top). They fired down into the troops. The crossed swords mark the place where "the principal part of the battle was fought."

Shown in this nineteenth–century illustration (opposite page), the first British soldiers fall as the Battle of the Wilderness begins. Surrounded by dense brush, the British were unable to see who was shooting at them. Their red coats made easy targets for the French and Indians.

Wounded in the battle, General Braddock is pictured (above) being carried away in a cart by his retreating troops. Braddock died four days later and was buried near Fort Necessity.

THE FRENCH AND BRITISH GENERALS

The French and Indian War began as a dispute over possession of the Ohio Valley. It became a fight to the death between Britain and France for control of North America. In 1756, the war became a world war. Fighting spread to Europe and to colonies in other regions, such as India and the West Indies. Other European countries took sides—Prussia with Britain; Austria, Russia, and Spain with France. In Europe, the war was called the Seven Years' War (because it lasted there from 1756 to 1763).

France won most of the early battles in America, beginning with Great Meadows and Braddock's defeat near Fort Duquesne a year later (1755). The Indian allies of the French attacked British settlements. Then, in 1758, a new British prime minister, William Pitt, changed the tide of war. He sent money, ships, and troops to America along with talented young officers. With the help of colonial soldiers and Iroquois allies, the British won battles in 1758 at Fort Frontenac, Louisbourg, and Fort Duquesne. In 1759, the British captured Quebec, the capital of New France. In 1760, Montreal fell to the British. When the European war ended in 1763, France signed away most of its North American possessions at the Peace of Paris. Britain was now the master of North America east of the Mississippi River.

General Jeffrey Amherst (1717-97; above) became the British commander-in-chief in America in 1758. Louis Joseph, the Marquis de Montcalm (1712-59; below), was commander-in-chief of French regular troops in Canada from 1756 to 1759.

This map (right) shows the locations of major battles in the French and Indian War. The war began in the Ohio River valley (inside the dotted area, marking present-day Pennsylvania). It ended at Quebec and Montreal in Canada, the largest cities of New France. Fighting also spread to the areas that were the three main approaches to Canada: the Great Lakes route (Fort Niagara), the Lake Champlain route (Crown Point, Ticonderoga), and the Gulf of St. Lawrence (Louisbourg).

Young James Wolfe (1727-59), shown here (below) proclaiming the deeds his sword would achieve in North America, was perhaps the most colorful officer appointed by Prime Minister Pitt.

THE BATTLE OF LAKE GEORGE

Most of the Indian tribes of the East and Midwest were allies of the French. But the British had one powerful ally—the Iroquois Confederacy. Of the six Iroquois nations, the most loyal to the British was the Mohawk. In1755, William Johnson led an army of three thousand colonists and five hundred Mohawks up the Hudson River in New York to "the Great Carrying Place." This was a portage trail—a land trail connecting the Hudson River and Lake George. (Lake George was important because it fed into Lake Champlain, on the border of Canada.) Johnson built Fort Edward on the Hudson River and marched on to Lake George, where he set up camp. Meanwhile, a force of thirty-two hundred regular French troops and Indian allies arrived in the area. On September 8, 1755, Mohawk scouts reported to Johnson that the enemy was near. Johnson sent a thousand men to investigate. They walked into an ambush: the first engagement of the Battle of Lake George. Many British and Iroquois were killed, including Mohawk chief Tiyanoga the Great. Fearing the worst, the British ringed their camp with muskets and artillery. When the French arrived, the British fired. The French fell in droves and the French commander was captured. Johnson's colonists were proud to have beaten a European army. They had won the first British victory in the war.

William Johnson (1715-74; above), New York landowner and trader, treated his Mohawk neighbors with fairness and respect. Johnson lived with a Mohawk woman named Molly Brant (1736-96) and took part in tribal councils. As superintendent of Indian affairs, Johnson helped to keep the Iroquois on the British side during the French and Indian War. For his victory at Lake George, he was appointed a baronet (nobleman).

The Mohawk chief Theyanoguin (c. 1680-1755; right) was also called King Hendrick or "Tiyanoga the Great." After converting to Christianity early in his life, he became a preacher and a staunch ally of the British. He even visited England in 1710, along with three other Indian chiefs and colonial escorts. Tiyanoga was over seventy when he fought and died at Lake George.

This plan (below) of the Battle of Lake George shows the way troops were arranged. The two engagements took place at the trail connecting the Hudson River and Lake George (map, top). In the first engagement (left panel), British troops march into an ambush of French and Indians. In the second engagement (right panel), the French march into a blistering British defense.

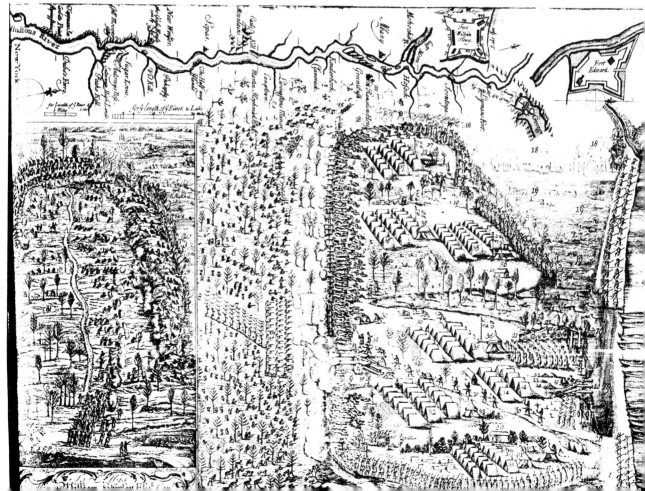

THE FRENCH SURRENDER LOUISBOURG

British ships surround the walled city of Louisbourg during the siege in 1758 (opposite page; bottom). At center is the city (with houses and church spires). In the foreground, at Lighthouse Point, the British direct the building of siege fortifications.

French and British fleets clash during the siege of Louisbourg (opposite page; above). Cannonballs fly and ships sink in this somewhat fanciful illustration.

Britain had captured the French fortress of Louisbourg in Nova Scotia in 1745, during King George's War, but had returned it to France at the end of the war. Now, in 1758, it had to be captured again. The fortified town of Louisbourg on Cape Breton Island was stronger than ever, defended by three thousand troops. Strategically, Louisbourg was extremely important as it guarded the approaches to the Gulf of St. Lawrence and the St. Lawrence River, and thus was the key to the control of Canada.

This time it was attacked not by a colonial army but by regular British troops and a fleet from the Royal Navy. About 150 warships and transports carried 25,000 men to Louisbourg. General Jeffrey Amherst was in charge. On June 8, 1758, the British attacked. The British army had a hard time coming ashore as the French fired cannons at their landing boats. But James Wolfe, the field commander, found a way onto the shore. The British laid siege to Louisbourg, surrounding it with artillery. They occupied Lighthouse Point across the harbor. British cannons bombarded Louisbourg, devastating the town. French warships in the harbor were burned or captured. On July 26, Louisbourg surrendered. The town and fortress were destroyed two years later.

AN ENGLISH VICTORY ON LAKE CHAMPLAIN

Stretching north-south between Canada and New York, Lake Champlain was the easiest route to the very heart of New France. Control of the lake was crucial to victory. But the guns of two French forts menaced the lake: Fort Carillon (called Ticonderoga by the British) and Fort St. Frèdèric at Crown Point. On July 8, 1758, British general James Abercrombie tried to get past the barricades defending Ticonderoga. His force of fifteen thousand troops was nearly five times larger than that of the French. But instead of using his artillery, Abercrombie foolishly ordered his men to charge the fort. Shooting from behind the barricades, the French cut down about two thousand men. One English soldier wrote mournfully, "For seven hours we fought the French, while we were all in open field and they within a trench." The next year, General Amherst attacked Ticonderoga with eight thousand men. He prepared carefully and moved slowly, determined not to repeat Abercrombie's mistakes. Expecting defeat, the French secretly abandoned the fort in July 1759—but not before blowing it up. The French also abandoned and destroyed their fort at Crown Point. In July and August, Amherst took possession of the ruins of the two forts.

After capturing Ticonderoga and Crown Point in 1759, General Amherst rebuilt the destroyed forts. The star-shaped plan of most colonial forts, shown in this diagram of Crown Point (opposite page; top), allowed the defenders to shoot at the approaching enemy from several angles at once, catching them in crossfire.

The French Fort Carillon (Ticonderoga) was built at the place where Lake George meets Lake Champlain (opposite page; bottom). By capturing the fort, the British gained control of one of the three approaches to Quebec. The others were via the Great Lakes and, most important, via the Gulf of St. Lawrence. The shaded areas on the map mark the slopes of high ground. Lines of French soldiers defended the fort at "N" in the upper left.

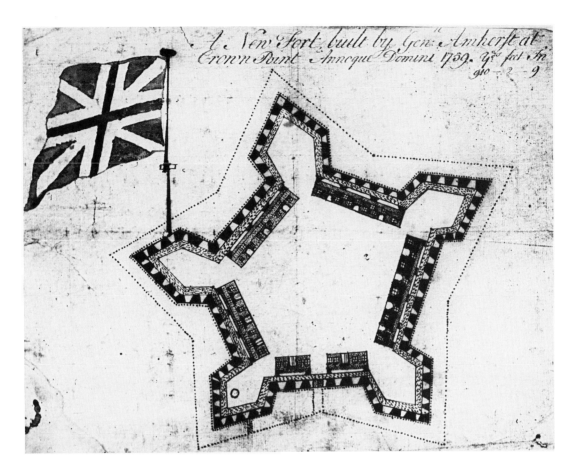

A New Fort built by Genl. Amherst at Crown Point Annoque Domini 1759. Ye fot In 910 – 2 – 9

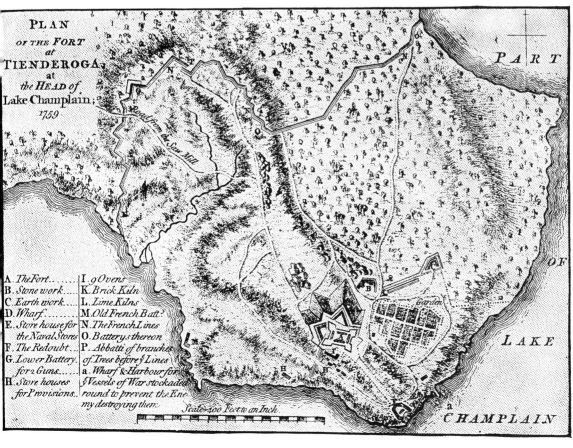

PLAN OF THE FORT at TIENDEROGA at the HEAD of Lake Champlain, 1759

PART

OF

LAKE

CHAMPLAIN

A. The Fort ....
B. Stone work ......
C. Earth work .....
D. Wharf ....
E. Store house for the Naval Stores
F. The Redoubt ...
G. Lower Battery for 2 Guns .....
H. Store houses for Provisions.

I. 9 Ovens
K. Brick Kiln
L. Lime Kilns
M. Old French Batt.?
N. The French Lines
O. Batterys thereon
P. Abbatti of branches of Trees before ye Lines
a. Wharf & Harbour for ye Vessels of War stockaded round to prevent the Enemy destroying them.

Scale 400 Feet to an Inch

THE BATTLE OF QUEBEC

Quebec, the capital of New France, was built on cliffs along the St. Lawrence River. Its strong natural defenses had been reinforced in 1759 by General Montcalm's fifteen thousand troops. To win the war, the British had to capture this city. In June 1759, a fleet of about two hundred British ships arrived just east of Quebec. General James Wolfe secured an island called the Isle d'Orléans as a base for his nine thousand troops. Throughout the summer, British artillery from Point Levi on the opposite bank bombarded Quebec. In the countryside, British patrols burned houses and farmland. Civilians were terrified, but the French army did not move. Finally, on September 13, 1759, Wolfe forced them into battle.

Just before dawn, British troops overpowered the militia who guarded a narrow trail up the cliffs west of Quebec. Within hours, forty-five hundred British troops stood in ranks outside the city walls, daring the French to come out and fight. Montcalm took the dare. The two sides, about equal in numbers, joined battle on the Plains of Abraham. Hundreds died on both sides, including Wolfe and Montcalm. But British discipline was better, and the French were routed. Quebec surrendered a few days later. When Montreal was captured the next year (September 8, 1760), New France fell into British hands.

On September 13, 1759, General Wolfe's forces attacked Quebec. This drawing (above) compresses several different parts of the battle into one scene. In the lower left, British soldiers scramble up the cliffs, exchanging fire with Canadian militia while boats land troops. Hours later, on the Plains of Abraham above the cliffs, the British and French armies meet in battle.

As Wolfe lies dying on the Plains of Abraham (above), a British soldier tells him, "They run!" "Who runs?" asks Wolfe. "The enemy, sir!" says the soldier. The young general's death as he led his troops to victory captured the imagination of British and Americans alike.

Montcalm took longer to die than Wolfe. Here (opposite page; above) he lies on his sickbed in the French camp, shot in the stomach. He died early on the morning of September 14, 1759. He was buried in a convent, in a hole caused by British shelling.

This cartoon (opposite page; below) celebrates the British victory in America. Britain is seen as having defended its "rights" while curbing French "ambition." (A French cartoonist might have talked about French "rights" and British "ambition.") On the left is Britannia (Britain) with the Roman gods Mars (war) and Neptune (ocean). On the right, a weeping "Genius" (spirit) of France stands with a dismayed French politician while Jack Tar (a British sailor) sneers at them.

PONTIAC'S REBELLION

The British colonists were happy to see New France defeated, but most Indians were not. The French had treated their Indian allies with respect, giving them gifts and keeping their lands free from settlers. The British who took over French forts in the Great Lakes region (the "west") did not treat them as well. In the spring of 1763, with the help of some of the remaining Frenchmen, the western Indian tribes rebelled. The rebellion is named for Pontiac (c. 1720-69), an Ottawa chief, but he was probably not the sole leader. The Indians captured most of the western posts and ravaged settlements from New York to Virginia. The British fought back. The commander of Fort Pitt even used a kind of germ warfare, giving the Indians blankets contaminated with smallpox, a deadly disease. In 1764, most of the Indian tribes made peace, although Pontiac did not surrender until 1766. Pontiac was killed in 1769 by another Indian.

During the French and Indian War, some colonists learned to adopt Indian techniques of forest warfare. One of these colonists was Robert Rogers (1731-95; above), who formed a company called Rogers's Rangers and helped defend Fort Detroit.

Not every Indian joined Pontiac's Rebellion. This Abenaki chief is rescuing an English officer from hostile braves (below).

Rogers (above) met Pontiac while on his way to take over Fort Detroit.

Colonel Henry Bouquet (1719-65) discusses terms for the Indians' surrender (below).

Resource Guide

Key to picture positions: (T) top, (C) center,
(B) bottom; and in combinations: (TL) top left,
(TC) top center, (TR) top right, (BL) bottom left,
(BC) bottom center, (BR) bottom right,
(CR) center right, (CL) center left.

Key to picture locations within the Library of
Congress collections (and where available,
photo-negative numbers): P - Prints and
Photographs; HABS - Historical American Buildings
Survey (div. of Prints and Photographs); R - Rare
Book Division; G - General Collections; MSS -
Manuscript Division; G&M - Geography and
Map Division.

PICTURES IN THIS VOLUME

2-3 Crown Point, P, USZ62-49009 4-5 soldiers, G 6-7
Philip, P, USZ62-96234 8-9 attack, P, USZ62-675

Timeline I:
10 Luther, G 11 T, ships, G; C, Drake, G; B, totem G 12
T, Gustavus, G; B, houses, G 13 T, execution, G; C,
Stuyvesant, G; B, New Amsterdam, G 14-15
map, G 16-17 TL, De Soto, P, USZ62-354; TR,
Indians, P, USZ62-33888; BR, camp, P, USZ62-3034
18-19 TR, Outina, R; BR, village, R 20-21 BL, St.
Augustine; TR, Huguenots, G; BR, murder, R 22-
23 TL, title page, R; BR, map, P, USZ62-9285 24-25
attack, P, USZ62-77106 26-27 TL, warrior, P,
USZ62-60373; BL, trading, G; BR, fort, P, USZ62-
33988 28-29 TL, title page, P, USZ62-57966; BL,
warrior, R; TR, map, P, USZ62-9287 30-31 TL,
Powhatan, P, USZ62-31735; BL, chief, R; TR, village,
R 32-33 TL, massacre, P, USZ62-32377; TR, capture,
G 34-35 TL, Wassaquisett, G; TR, letter, G; BR,
Pilgrims, P, USZ62-21923 36-37 TR, map, G; BR,
fort, P, USZ62-32055 38-39 TL, Fort Trinity, R; BL,
siege, R; TR, map, P, USZ62-5140; BR, trading, G 40-
41 TL, title page, P, USZ62-5141; BL, army, P,
USZ62-84371; TR, map, R; BR, Stuyvesant, P,
USZ62-13439 42-43 TR, treaty, P, USZ62-49461;
BR, map, G 44-45 TL, Church, P, USZ62-96233; BL,
fighting, P, USZ62-42821; TR, bayonets, P, USZ62-
32069; BR, title page, R 46-47 TL, title page, R; TR,
swamp fight, G; BR, death, G 48-49 Quebec, G&M

Timeline II:
50 T, Newton, G; C, La Salle, G; B, Seal, G 51 T,
Marlborough, G; C, St. Augustine, P, USZ62-053276;
B, cottage, P 52 T, Frederick, G; C, woman and child,
P, USZ62-30729; B, title page, MSS 53 T, Charles
Edward, G; C, Oglethorpe, P, USZ62-1922; B,
Moravians, P,USZ62-21033 54-55 TL, King William,
P, USZ62-78296; TR, map, R; BR, ships, R 56-57 TL,
Queen Anne, G; BR, map, G&M 58-59 TL, Indian
house, HABS; BL, canoeing, P, USZ62-38424; TC,

block house, G; BC, palisaded house, G; TR, title page,
R 60-61 TL, Tomochichi, P, USZ62-1921; TR, map,
G&M; BR, Tuscaroras, G 62-63 TL, title page, MSS;
TR, Algonquins, G&M; BR, Yazoo, P, USZ62-30706
64-65 TL, La Salle, P; TR, newspaper, R; BR, map, R
66-67 TL, George II, G; TR, Pepperell, G; BR,
Louisbourg, R 68-69 TL, manual, P, USZ62-61163;
BL, victory, P, USZ62-21350; TR, plan, R 70-71
Wolfe, P, USZ62-48404

Timeline III:
72 T, Pitt, G; C, fort, G; B, Acadians, G 73 C, Wolfe, G;
B, flower, P 74-75 BL, soldier, G; TC, ledger, MSS;
TR, Washington, P, USZ62-4276 76-77 TL, Braddock,
P, USZ62-9703; BL, plan, R; TR, marching, G 78-79
TR, ambush, G; TR, wounded, P, USZ62-51691 80-81
TL, Amherst, P, USZ62-33518; BL, Montcalm, P,
USZ61-239; TR, map, G; BR, Wolfe, P, USZ62-20290
82-83 TL, Johnson, P, USZ62-2695; TR, Tiyanoga, P,
USZ62-45198; BR, plan, P, USZ62-22018 84-85 TR,
capture, P, USZ62-21295; BR, Louisbourg, P, USZ62-
2771 86-87 TR, Crown Point, G&M; BR, Ticonderoga,
R 88-89 Ile d'Orleans, P, USZ62-47 90-91 TL, Wolfe,
P, USZ62-111; TR, Montcalm, P, USZ62-106; BR,
cartoon, P, USZ62-1502 92-93 TL, Rogers, G; BL,
woodcut, P, USZ62-45552; TR, Pontiac, P, USZ62-
14142; BR, Bouquet, P, USZ62-103

SUGGESTED READING

DANIEL, CLIFTON. *Chronicle of America.* New York:
Prentice Hall, 1989.
DONOVAN, FRANK R. *The Many Worlds of Benjamin
Franklin.* Mahwah, N.J.: Troll Associates, 1963.
MORRISON, SAMUEL. *The Oxford History of the American
People.* New York: 1965.
OCHOA, GEORGE. *The Fall of Quebec.* New York: Silver
Burdett, 1990.

WRIGHT, LOUIS B. *The American Heritage History of the
Thirteen Colonies.* New York: Simon and Schuster,
1967.
ENCYCLOPEDIA BRITTANICA. *The Annals of America,* volume
2. Chicago: Encyclopedia Brittanica, Inc., 1976.

Index

Page numbers in *italics* indicate illustrations.